Visual Basic® 6

First Edition

Shimon Mordynski
Lowell Mauer

A Division of Macmillan Computer Publishing, USA
201 W. 103rd Street
Indianapolis, Indiana 46290

SAMS

Visually in **Full Color**

How to Use Visual Basic® 6

International Standard Book Number: 0-672-31443-6

Library of Congress Catalog Card Number: 98-86998

Printed in the United States of America

First Printing: December 1998

00   99   4   3   2

Executive Editor
Chris Denny

Acquisitions Editor
Sharon Cox

Development Editor
Todd Bumbalough

Managing Editor
Jodi Jensen

Project Editor
Maureen A. McDaniel

Copy Editor
Maureen A. McDaniel

Indexer
Charlotte Clapp

Proofreaders
Mona Brown
Michael Henry
Donna Martin

Technical Editors
Rob Bernavich
Dallas G. Releford

Software Development Specialist
Dan Scherf

Cover Designer
Karen Ruggles

Interior Designers
Nathan Clement
Ruth Harvey

Layout Technician
Trina Wurst

Contents at a Glance

Contents

About the Authors

Shimon Mordzynski is an independent consultant with 20 years experience in developing and designing systems and applications. He has designed and implemented management seminars and technical courses for personnel at a corporate level. His specialty is designing and implementing database applications working with planning and decision support management.

Lowell Mauer is a Senior Business Analyst for Cognos Corporation. As a manager of technical support, he has attended seminars and training sessions in several countries and is an expert in more than six computer languages. He supports several client/server products, as well as teaches and develops product workshops. Lowell has been a programmer and instructor for 20 years. He has taught programming at Montclair State College in New Jersey, has developed and marketed a Visual Basic application, and is involved in creating several corporate Web site applications. Lowell is the author of *Sams Teach Yourself More Visual Basic 6 in 21 Days* and has also contributed on several other books, such as *Visual Basic 6 Unleashed* and *Platinum Edition Using Visual Basic 5*. He has also been a technical editor for several books such as *Visual Basic 5 Night School* and *Special Edition Using Visual Basic 5*.

How To Use This Book

The Complete Visual Reference

Each chapter of this book is made up of a series of short, instructional tasks, designed to help you understand all the information that you need to get the most out of your computer hardware and software.

Click: Click the left mouse button once.

Double-click: Click the left mouse button twice in rapid succession.

Right-click: Click the right mouse button once.

Pointer Arrow: Highlights an item on the screen you need to point to or focus on in the step or task.

Selection: Highlights the area onscreen discussed in the step or task.

Click and Type: Click once where indicated and begin typing to enter your text or data.

Click & Drag

Release

How to Drag: Point to the starting place or object. Hold down the mouse button (right or left per instructions), move the mouse to the new location, and then release the button.

Key icons: Clearly indicate which key combinations to use.

Each task includes a series of easy-to-understand steps designed to guide you through the procedure.

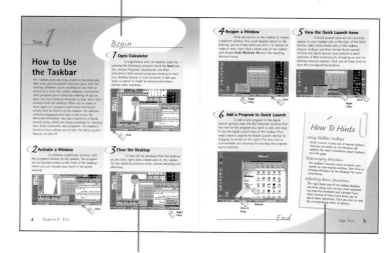

Each step is fully illustrated to show you how it looks onscreen.

Extra hints that tell you how to accomplish a goal are provided in most tasks.

Menus and items you click are shown in **bold**. Words in *italic* are defined in more detail in the glossary. Information you type is in a **special font**.

Continues

If you see this symbol, it means the task you're in continues on the next page.

Introduction

*W*elcome to the programming world of Visual Basic. Learning how to program, or instruct the computer in how to perform its tasks, is one of the most satisfying and frustrating skills you will ever learn. Many people think that learning how to create programs for a computer is a life-long task. However, everyone has to start someplace. With Visual Basic, the task of learning has become somewhat easier.

For those of you who just want to find out what programming is all about or want to get started slowly because of time, there is a way. Using Visual Basic and this book will allow you to learn many of the features of Visual Basic that you can use to create applications for your computer. Using Visual Basic requires that you learn about the interface before actually creating an application. In the first couple of chapters in this book, you will learn the following:

✓ How to install Visual Basic

✓ The parts of the Visual Basic interface

✓ What makes up a Visual Basic project

✓ How to start your first application project

Once you have gotten a feel for what it takes to start a project in Visual Basic, you will then learn some of the more common features of the standard basic language that you will use when coding your application. This includes concepts that show you the following:

✓ How to define variables

✓ How to use the If statement

✓ How to use the Select statement

✓ How to use the Do loop

✓ How to find errors in the application

✓ How to use common controls on a form

✓ How to work with data files

Whether you have just started working with a computer and want to learn how to program it, or have been using computers for years and want to know a little bit more about how they actually work, Visual Basic 6 will show you. Learning a new language can be very scary by itself. But, learning a new language that will command a computer is even worse. That's why *How to Use Visual Basic 6* provides concise, visual, step-by-step instructions for working with all the standard features of Visual Basic 6 that you need to create an application. These include learning how to use the different building blocks of Visual Basic, such as the following:

✓ Textboxes

✓ Command buttons

✓ Labels

✓ Frames

✓ Option buttons

In addition, you will also learn how to use some of the more advanced controls to interact with the user. These include

✓ MonthView

✓ Animation

✓ StatusBar

✓ ProgressBar

✓ Tab Dialog

✓ Common Dialog

The *How to Use* series provides pictures of the Visual Basic screens to show you what you will see in each step of a task and explains the process without boring you with complicated explanations. In plain English, and using no more than seven steps per task, *How to Use Visual Basic 6* shows you what it takes to create a working Windows application.

And just in case you are feeling ambitious, *How to Use Visual Basic 6* provides seven Project sections, designed to illustrate in 20-something easy steps how to complete an entire project. For example, the Project in Chapter 5, "Changing the Project's Interface," steps you through the creation of a complete menu and toolbar for an application. And the one in Chapter 18, "Working with Simple Files," illustrates how to read and write data to a file on the computer.

Besides the basics of using Visual Basic, you will also see how to access information from a database, such as Microsoft Access or Oracle. Then in Chapter 20, "Using Visual Basic Add-Ins," you are introduced to some of the wizards and add-ins that come with Visual Basic that help to make the development process easier, including the following:

- ✓ Application Wizard
- ✓ Toolbar Wizard
- ✓ Data Form Wizard
- ✓ Visual Data Manager
- ✓ API Viewer
- ✓ Template Manager

Finally, you can choose to read *How to Use Visual Basic 6* cover to cover, or to use it as a reference as you start using Visual Basic 6. Either way, *How to Use Visual Basic 6* has been carefully designed to ensure that you get all the information you need to get started with Visual Basic. In addition, the *How to Use* series provides an extra layer of information called How-To Hints for most tasks.

No matter how you use *How to Use Visual Basic 6*, you will be up and running in no time flat. So invest a little bit of time learning how to use Visual Basic...you'll be glad you did!

Task

1

Getting Started with Visual Basic 6

*N*ow that you have taken the plunge and purchased Visual Basic 6, you are probably wondering where to start. Well, the best place to start is the beginning. What is Visual Basic? Visual Basic is the best-known and most widely used Windows programming language today. It provides you with a way of creating Windows applications without having to learn any strange, complicated language like C++. By using the point-and-click method, Visual Basic lets you "draw" your application and then add any code that is needed.

This chapter introduces you to a few key concepts about what a Windows application really consists of and how to get started by installing the Visual Basic product. It explains some of the different options that you can choose during the install process, as well as how to install the MSDN product which includes all of the Visual Basic Help files. Finally, you will see how to start Visual Basic and where to find help when you need it. ●

Understanding Windows Programming

Before you start learning about Visual Basic, you must first understand what makes a Windows application really work. If you have been using Windows for any length of time, you probably know more than you think. However, by taking a quick look at a simple and very familiar application, you will see how it interacts with the Windows operating system.

Begin

1 Open the Calculator

Start the Calculator by clicking the **Start** button, choosing **Programs** and **Accessories**, and then choosing **Calculator**.

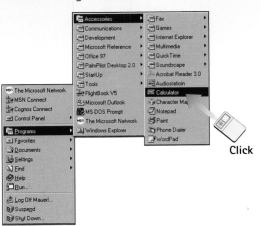

Click

2 Common Objects in an Application

Whenever an application is started, it displays a main form that you, as the user, will interact with. The **Calculator** contains many of the standard elements included on its form.

Menu

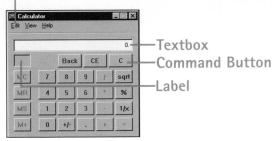

Textbox
Command Button
Label

3 Events Make It Happen

Everything you do in a Windows application causes something called an *event*. An event occurs when you type something into a textbox, click a command button, or by hundreds of other reasons. Click one of the number buttons on the **Calculator**. You will see that a number appears in the textbox.

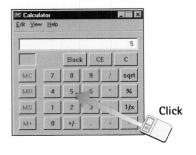

Click

4 Events Working by Themselves

Events even let you perform actions in your application when the user is doing nothing. You have seen these events in word processing, such as an AutoSave feature, or in Windows itself, such as a clock.

5 Automatic Properties

Even when you do not change properties in your code, they are being changed whenever the user clicks an object in the program.

End

How-To Hints

Events

Events are the basic process by which Windows "knows" what is happening in a program. An event can be anything the user does, such as pressing a key, moving the mouse, clicking objects, and so on. Your programs are expected to understand what the user just did and react to it.

Methods

A method is really a built-in function that was defined and coded by Microsoft to provide an action that you can use for that object.

Properties

A property is an attribute of a control, field, or database object that you set to define one of the object's characteristics or an aspect of its behavior. In addition, you can always display the current value of a property.

How to Install Visual Basic 6

Even before using Visual Basic, you must install it on your computer. Although Visual Basic 6 is included in Visual Studio 98, it is also sold separately. When you install Visual Basic 6, there are many options that you can select that will affect what you can and cannot use in Visual Basic on your computer.

Begin

1 Insert the CD

These days most products are distributed on CD-ROM and have something called *AutoPlay* enabled on them. This means that the product install process will automatically start when you place the CD into the computer's CD reader.

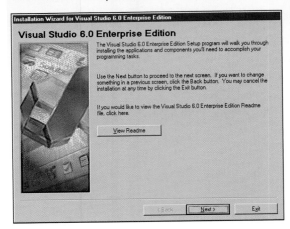

2 Enter the Product Number

Every Microsoft product that you install will require you to enter an ID number that can be found in the back of the CD's case.

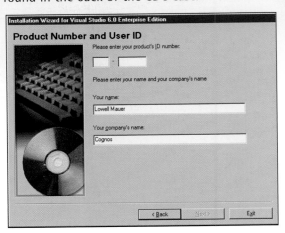

3 Select the Setup Options

Once you have entered the ID number, the next step is to choose what you want to install.

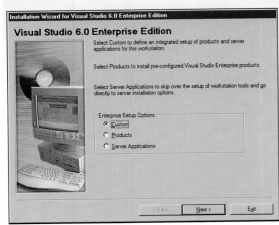

4 The Common Install Folder

During the installation process, there will be many programs and support files that are used by more than just Visual Basic. These are installed to the common folder that you specify on this dialog form.

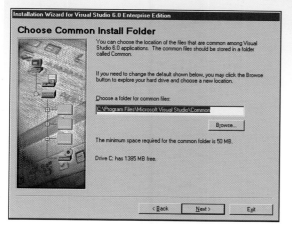

5 Choose the Install Options

The last step in the process is to choose the options that you want to install. If you are unsure of what to choose, the default options will get you started.

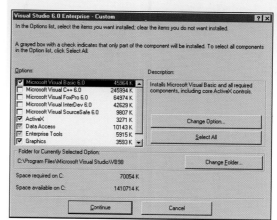

6 Finish the Install

After Visual Basic has been installed, you must restart your computer. By clicking the **Restart Windows** button, the install program will do this for you.

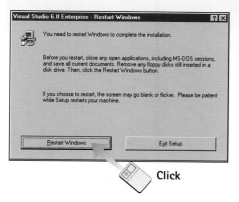

Click

End

How-To Hints

Available Space

Before starting the install process, you should make sure that there is enough space available on the hard drive you want to install Visual Basic on. The average amount of space required to install Visual Basic is approximately 150MB.

Additional Installations

In addition to Visual Basic, the latest version of Internet Explorer 4.01 must be installed in order for some of the new features of Visual Basic 6 to be installed properly.

How to Install MSDN Help

Once the Visual Basic product is installed, you will be asked if you want to install the Microsoft Developers Network (MSDN) Help software and support files. In addition, there are several other product installations that you will be asked about.

Begin

1 Start the Install

Although the MSDN install process is started automatically, it still requires you to click the **Install MSDN** checkbox to actually install the software.

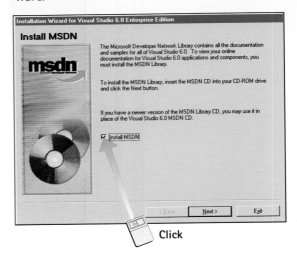

Click

2 Choose the Install Options

As with Visual Basic, you can select from several installation options. In addition, you can specify where to install the software. Click the **Typical** install button to continue.

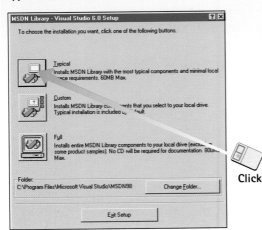

Click

3 Select the Components

When installing MSDN, you can select from many different Help file systems as well as a few search options. Choose the first three options for Visual Basic and click **Continue**.

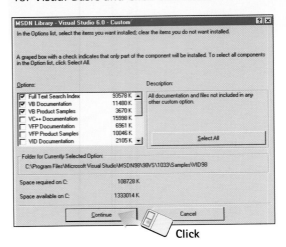

Click

4 Other Tools to Install

Visual Basic comes with one or more additional client tools that you can install.

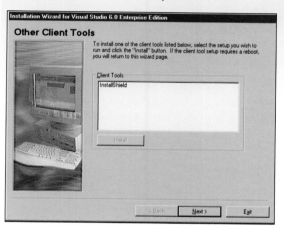

5 Server Setup Options

Finally, there are also a few server options you can choose to install, such as Visual SourceSafe.

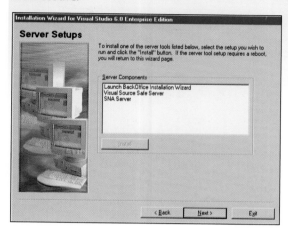

6 Register Visual Basic

The last step in this entire process is to register Visual Basic with Microsoft.

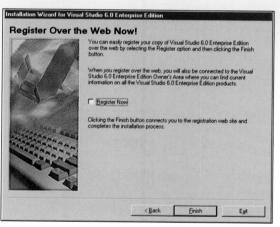

End

How-To Hints

Available Space

When installing MSDN, you can choose to install the entire set of Help files to your PC. However, it takes over 800MB to do this. For most users, the **Typical** install is enough.

How to Get Started in Visual Basic 6

Getting started with Visual Basic is as simple as any other application. You first start the application and then, using the functions and features that are available to you within the product, you create a Windows application to perform some predetermined task or set of tasks. The Visual Basic environment consists of many unique tools and windows that you will use to develop the application. In this task, you will learn about the options that are available when Visual Basic is started.

Begin

1 Start Visual Basic

You would start Visual Basic by clicking the **Start** button, choosing **Programs** and **Microsoft Visual Studio 6.0**, and then choosing **Microsoft Visual Basic 6.0**.

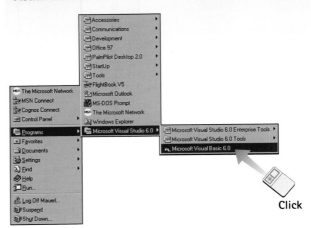

Click

2 The New Project Dialog

When Visual Basic first opens, you will see the **New Project** dialog displayed in the center of the screen. You can choose to start a new project, select an existing one, or choose from a list of projects you have recently used. For this task, select the **Standard EXE** icon from the **New** tab and click the **Open** button.

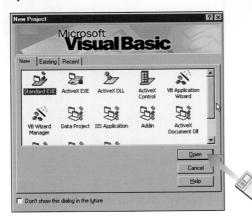

Click

3 The Default Project

Once you have selected the standard EXE project, the Visual Basic environment displays the default project. This project will contain an empty form which is named Form1. In the following chapters, you will learn how to add objects to this form and how to change its name and other properties.

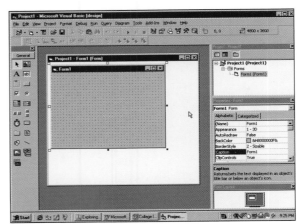

4 The Visual Basic Workarea

The Visual Basic environment contains several windows that will serve very specific functions in the development process. At the top of the screen, you can see Visual Basic's menu and toolbars.

5 The Toolbox

The toolbox displays buttons that represent the controls that are available for you to add to a form. Three of the most commonly used controls in Visual Basic are labels, textboxes, and command buttons.

Label
Textbox
Command Button

6 The Project Explorer

Another useful window is the **Project Explorer**. This is where every form and code module you add to the project are listed. In addition, other more advanced objects, such as a Custom control and Data Reports, are listed in this window.

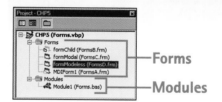

Forms
Modules

End

How-To Hints

Adding Forms to the Project

Forms can be added to the project by choosing **Project, Add Form** from the menu. This will display a new empty form in your project and add it to the **Project Explorer**.

Exiting from Visual Basic

You should get into the habit of saving your changes before exiting Visual Basic. However, when you exit Visual Basic, you will be asked to save the changes you made to the open project before Visual Basic actually shuts down.

How to Get Help

Visual Basic has a complete and well-organized online help system included with it. As you develop the components of an application, you will be able to find detailed help on any specific object and its properties, methods, and events. This even includes examples of how to use them. In addition, when you are actually writing the code for your project, you can get instant help on any keyword in the Visual Basic programming language. As you might expect, the F1 function key is used to access help; wherever you are in the Visual Basic development environment, F1 will get you to help.

Begin

1 The Help Interface

Starting with Visual Basic 6, there is a new interface for the Help information. If you have ever used the MSDN software or network before, you should be familiar with this format. To start Help, you can either choose **Help** and **Contents** from the Visual Basic menu or start the **MSDN Help Library** independently of Visual Basic. Either way, the main help form is displayed.

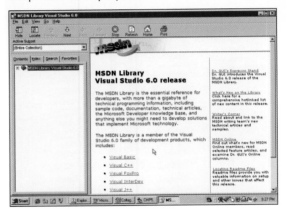

2 The Parts of Help

The help interface contains two main areas. The first area gives you the ability to search through the help files for a specific topic, and the second, larger area is where those files will be displayed.

3 Use the F1 Function Key

For a complete description of any control on a form, select the control in the form and press **F1**. The Visual Basic Help window will be displayed, providing the detailed information about the control you've selected.

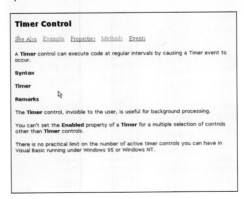

4 List a Control's Properties

Once you are viewing a help topic for a control, you can view the list of all the properties that apply to that control. To display this list, click the underlined word **Properties** at the top of the help topic. Then, select the property you want to read about from the list that is displayed. When you are finished reading about the property, click the **Back** button at the top of the form.

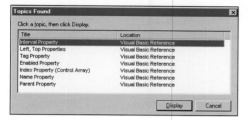

5 List a Control's Methods

Once you are viewing a help topic for a control, you can view the list of all the methods that apply to that control. To display this list, click the underlined word **Methods** at the top of the help topic. Then, select the method you want to read about from the list that is displayed. When you are finished, click the **Back** button at the top of the form.

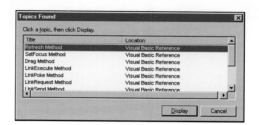

6 Finding a Topic

The Help libraries are organized into groups of related topics that are displayed as books on the **Contents** tab of the Help interface. This display allows you to open the books and browse the topics and chapters that are in them—giving you a quick way to browse a large list of help topics.

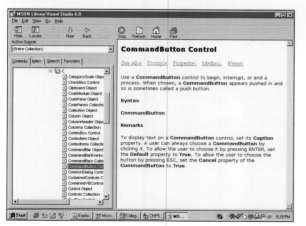

How-To Hints

Another Use of the F1 Function Key

Another way to get information about a property is to select an item in the **Properties** window and then press the **F1** key. This will display the help topic for the property you have selected.

End

Task

2

Introducing the
Visual Basic Interface

Now that you have installed Visual Basic, the sample projects, and the MSDN Help system libraries, you need to know a little about the interface you will be using. Besides the interface, you will also discover the different options you can set to customize the interface to your own liking. Using Visual Basic to develop a Windows application requires you to use many VB options and features to get the information you need to create a good, well-designed application.

In addition, you will learn how to add new controls to the **Toolbox**, as well as designers and insertable objects to your project. You will see how to use the **Object Browser**, which shows you all of the methods, properties, events, and constants that are available to you, depending on the reference libraries that are included in the project. ●

The Parts of the Interface

The Visual Basic interface is really comprised of many smaller dialog forms that can be displayed onscreen. These dialogs give you the ability to control everything that you need in your application. This task is going to show you each of the dialogs that you will be using most when developing a Visual Basic application.

Begin

1 Working with the Project Explorer

The **Project Explorer** is one of the most important dialogs that you will use in Visual Basic. This dialog displays all of the forms, modules, custom controls, property pages, and designers that you might have added to the project. By right-clicking in the **Project Explorer**, you will see a pop-up menu displayed that gives you the ability to maintain the objects in the project.

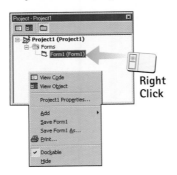

2 Display an Object's Properties

Whenever an object is active in Visual Basic, the **Properties window** lists all of the properties that are associated with that object. When you first display a form, the form is active by default and its properties are displayed in the **Properties window**.

3 Use the Form Layout Dialog

When you start working on a form in your application, you might want to specify where on the actual screen it will be displayed. You can do this by setting the form's **Top** and **Left** properties. However, you can do it visually by moving the image of the form in the **Form Layout** dialog, which shows the form in its actual position on the screen.

4 The Main Toolbars, Part I

Visual Basic has four toolbars that you can use to work with your project while designing the forms and adding the program code. The first two give you the **Standard** and **Edit** features and are the default toolbars that are displayed in the Visual Basic interface. The **Standard** toolbar contains functions such as **New Project**, **Add a Form**, **Open Project**, **Save Project**, and more. The Edit toolbar provides functions that are used in the Code Edit window, such as **Indent** and **Set Comment**.

5 The Main Toolbars, Part II

The other two toolbars that are available must be displayed by you. These include the **Debug** toolbar, which you will learn about later in this book, and the **Form Editor** toolbar, which gives you functions to help design the forms, such as align controls.

6 Use the Data View Dialog

The **Data View** dialog displays any of the data link or data environment connections that have been defined for your application. Either of these objects can be used to access data in a database such as Microsoft Access or Microsoft SQL Server.

End

How-To Hints

Docking the Dialogs

By default, the **Project Explorer**, **Properties window**, and **Form Layout** window are docked on the right side of the screen, while the **Toolbox** is docked on the left side. Unless you want to constantly move the dialogs around so that you can get to the forms you are creating, you should leave them where they are.

Toolbars

Although having all of the toolbars on the screen might sound like a good idea, unless you really need them you should only display the **Standard** and **Edit** toolbars.

How to Customize the Interface

The Visual Basic interface can be customized to suit the way you work. This means that if you feel that you do not need the **Auto List Members** function, you can turn it off. Or if you think the words are too small, you can change the font size in the **Code Editor**. There are quite a number of features and settings that you can control in Visual Basic; however, before you start playing with them, you should understand the basic concept behind them.

Begin

1 Display the Visual Basic Options

Displaying the Visual Basic interface options is done by choosing **Tools**, **Options** from the main Visual Basic menu bar.

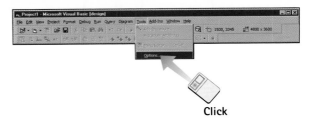

Click

2 Set the Edit Options

The **Editor** tab allows you to turn on or off many of the features that you can use in the **Code Editor**. This includes automatic syntax checking and auto indenting. You should check how each of these settings affects the way you use the **Code Editor** and then choose those options you want to keep.

3 Change the Code Editor Format

Like any other text editor, you have the ability to change the **Font**, **Size**, and **Code Colors** in the **Code Editor**.

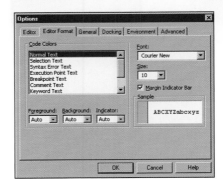

4 The General Options

The options that are listed on the **General** tab affect the way you can place objects on a form, how Visual Basic deals with an error that occurs during the execution of the project, and how the project is compiled when you are testing it.

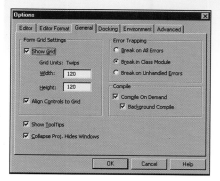

5 How the Dialogs Are Docked

In the previous task, you saw the different dialogs that you have access to in the Visual Basic project. The **Docking** tab allows you to specify which dialogs are allowed to be docked on the screen.

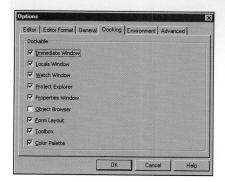

6 Modify the Environment

You can also specify how you want Visual Basic to act when it starts and when you start the execution of a project. In addition, you can tell Visual Basic which types of templates you want to see when you are adding an object to the project. The **Environment** tab lists all of the available templates and startup options.

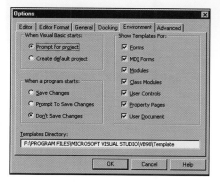

End

How-To Hints

Changing the Defaults

Although you can change any or all of the option settings for the Visual Basic interface and environment, you should really take it slow when doing it. Try changing a few options to see what happens. Actually, the default settings are pretty good and you can get by without really changing them.

How to Add Controls to the Toolbox

The **Toolbox** on the left side of the Visual Basic interface contains all of the controls and objects that you can add to a form in your application. However, when you start a new project, the **Toolbox** only contains the standard controls that Visual Basic uses, such as the **Textbox** and the **Label** controls. As your applications become more complex or you want to use some of the more interesting controls, you must first add them to the **Toolbox** yourself.

Begin

1 Display the Components Dialog

The **Components** dialog contains three tabs that list all of the available controls, designers, and objects that you can add to the project. To display it, choose **Project**, **Components** from the main Visual Basic menu.

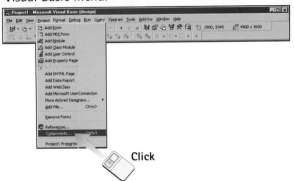

Click

2 Select the Controls to Include

The **Controls** tab lists every standard control, as well as any ActiveX control that has been installed on your computer. However, the only controls that you can really use in your project are those that came with Visual Basic or that you have purchased to use with Visual Basic. Other controls listed will not work in a development environment. Unfortunately, the only way for you to tell the difference is to attempt to add it to the project.

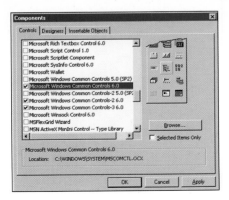

3 Add Designers to the Project

Visual Basic 6 comes with several advanced designers that help you create many of the objects, connections, or forms that you would use in a project. The **Designers** tab lists the available designers for you to choose from.

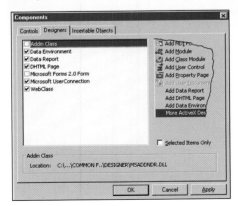

4 Other Objects to Include

Insertable objects are really any other application that you have installed on your computer that supports OLE processing. The **Insertable Objects** tab allows you to add objects such as a Word document to your application.

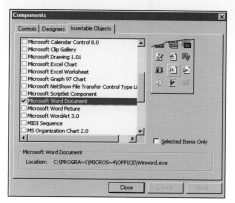

5 Add More Tabs to the Toolbox

As you add more controls to the **Toolbox**, it can become very crowded and displays many of the controls off the bottom of it. Or the **Toolbox** may become too large to work with. To prevent this, you can add more tabs to the **Toolbox** to group the controls and reduce the overall size of the **Toolbox**. To add a tab, you would right-click the **Toolbox**, choose **Add Tab**, and then enter the new tab name.

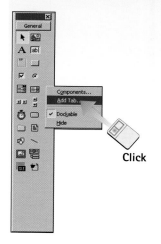

Click

6 Working with a New Tab

Once you have added a new tab to the **Toolbox**, you can move controls to that tab by dragging the control to the tab button and dropping it. To move between tabs, you would simply click the tab you need.

Click

How-To Hints

Selecting an Invalid Control

If you select a control that is not available in a development environment, you will receive an error message from Visual Basic the first time you try to add it to a form.

End

How to Use Reference Libraries and the Object Browser

The way Visual Basic provides you with the tips and syntax of the commands, methods, properties, and constants is by using something called reference libraries. Most ActiveX controls and other objects provide their own reference library for Visual Basic to use. In this task, you learn how to add a new reference library to your project and then how to look at what is in that library.

Begin

1 Display the Reference Library

To add a new reference library to your project, you would use the **References** dialog by choosing **Project**, **References** from the Visual Basic main menu.

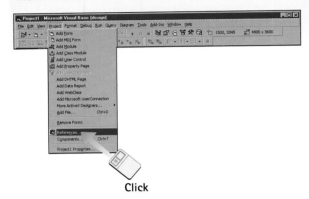

Click

2 Select the Reference Libraries

A reference library can be called either a type library or a DLL file that contains information about one or more objects that it is associated with. To add a library to your project, select the ones that you want by clicking the checkbox next to the name of the library.

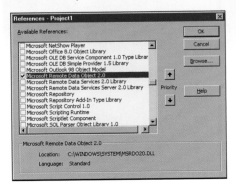

3 Display the Object Browser

Once you have added the reference libraries you need in your project, the only way to view what is in them is by using the **Object Browser** that comes with Visual Basic. The **Object Browser** is displayed by choosing **View**, **Object Browser** from the Visual Basic main menu.

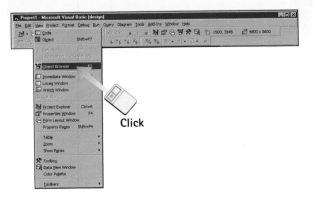

Click

4 Choose a Library to View

The **Object Browser** lists the objects from all of the libraries as the default. If you want to select a particular library, you would select it from the library drop-down list at the top of the browser.

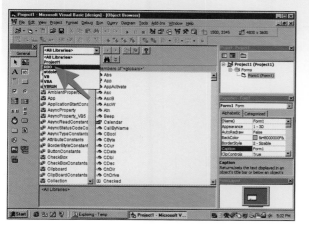

5 The Objects in a Library

Once you have selected a library and have found the object you want more information about, select it by clicking it. The **Object Browser** then lists the methods, properties, and events that are associated with the object. If you select one of the object's elements, a description of that element is displayed at the bottom of the **Object Browser**.

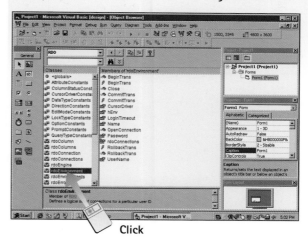

Click

6 Finding Constants

Visual Basic has already defined to it many of the constants' values that you use within the application. The **Object Browser** can be used to find a particular constant when needed.

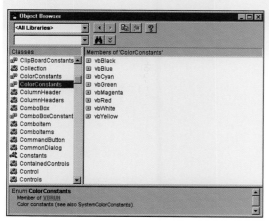

How-To Hints

Reference Libraries

Reference libraries can be used to include functionality from other applications on your computer, such as Excel or Word. By including the reference libraries for these applications, your Visual Basic application can execute commands within Excel or Word without requiring the user to start these applications themselves.

Object Browser

The **Object Browser** is an excellent way of finding out the different commands that are available to you from a particular reference library.

End

Task

3

Starting Your First Project

Embarking on your first Visual Basic project can be very intimidating. In fact, Visual Basic has so many options and features built into it that you might never use some of the more advanced ones. In this chapter, you are introduced to the tools and capabilities you can use in Visual Basic. In addition, you will see how to add controls and coding to your form. You will also review how to save and run your application. ●

How to Start and Save a New Project

After Visual Basic has started, select the type of project you want to create from the new project dialog screen. Selecting the **Standard EXE** option on the new tab and clicking the **Open** button displays a new default project for development. This environment is known as a design-time environment, where you design your screens and enter your code for the application.

Begin

1 The Form Screen

In the project, the default form should be recognizable as a standard window screen. The form screen is the graphical drawing pad of your project. The form contains grid dots to help you align your controls. Forms are used as display windows to gather information and return commands or instructions.

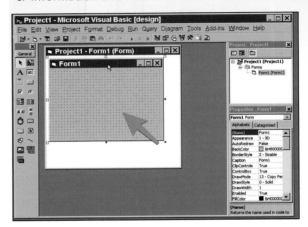

2 Save Your Work

It is good practice to save your work periodically. When you save your project for the first time, each item in the **Project Explorer** window will be saved. Each item refers to each component of your project, each form, and each module, as well as the project to be saved. To do a save, select the **Save Project** or **Save Project As** option under the **File** menu.

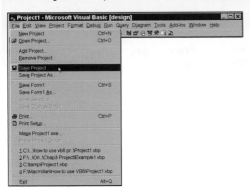

3 Project

Every time a project is saved, a project file (.VBP) gets updated. This file contains project descriptions and settings.

4 Forms

Along with the project file, Visual Basic creates a form module (.FRM) for each form in your application. This file contains the description and settings of each form.

5 Save as Option

The **Save Project As** option allows you to save your project and its items to new names. You can even create a new folder from this screen.

6 Toolbars

The **Toolbar** provides a quick access to the most frequently used commands during development. As you can see, **Open**, **Save**, and **Run** are readily available on the **Toolbar**.

End

How-To Hints

Focus

When a form is selected or "has the focus," it will have squares around the form. Likewise, when there are multiple objects on a form, the item that has the focus will have squares around it.

Saving Your Work

It is good practice to create separate folders for each project that you are working on. This allows for easier control of different forms and objects associated with each application.

After the project has been saved for the first time, the **Save Project** option will save all the components at once. It will prompt you for new names if you have added new items to the project.

How to Customize the Project Properties

When you begin a new application, it will have a default set of properties associated with it. When you access the **Project Properties**, there will be tabs with different options in each. For your purposes, you will not need to change very many options of the **Project Properties**. This task examines what **Project Properties** are and which ones you can change.

Begin

1 Access the Project Properties

The Project Properties dialog box is displayed by choosing **Project**, **<project name> Properties** from the main Visual Basic menu.

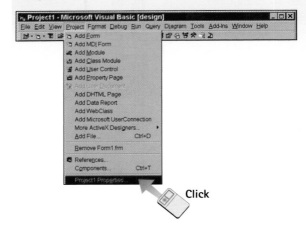

Click

2 The General Tab

Under the **General** tab, select the **Project Type**, **Project Name**, and **Project Description** options. So far you are only using the Standard EXE type. However, you may want to add a description or change the name. The most important item that you can change here is the **Startup Object**. This will tell Visual Basic which object should be run first at startup.

3 The Make Tab

The **Make** tab allows you to assign a name and an icon to the application. It also enables you to set a **Version Number**. **Version Information** lets you provide specific information about the current version of your project, such as your company name, file description, legal copyright, legal trademarks, product name, and comments.

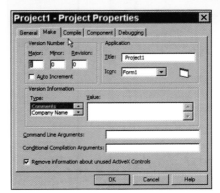

4 The Compile Tab

The **Compile** tab enables you to determine how your application should be compiled. There a two options—**Compile to P-Code** and **Compile to Native Code**. These options allow you to create an application that is optimized for the type of computer it will be running on. P-code, or pseudocode, will generate an application which uses an intermediate step to process the application. At runtime, Visual Basic translates each p-code statement to native code. By compiling directly to native code format, you eliminate the intermediate p-code step. For now, it's best to go with the default values that are supplied by Visual Basic.

End

How-To Hints

Application Version

Using the **Version Number** option is extremely helpful when you are supporting an existing version while making changes to the application. Also, when multiple versions of an application are being used, it is imperative that version numbers exist so that proper support is provided.

Properties

At this point, it's best to not change most of the properties. However, the **General** tab and the **Make** tab have properties that you set that can be used in your application. In fact, when you add a new form to your application and you want to test the new form, you should change the **Startup Object** in the **General** tab. When you start your application, your new form will be displayed at startup.

How to Add Controls to a Form

As previously mentioned, the form acts as a drawing pad and eventually becomes the visual result of your application. The **Toolbox** allows you to design your form with predefined objects. Visual Basic also supports graphical output on forms; this allows additional customization of your application.

Begin

1 Objects in the Toolbox

When your mouse pointer rests on a button in the **Toolbox**, a ToolTip box is displayed that identifies the control.

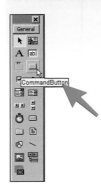

2 Select a Control

Clicking a control selects that item as being active. After selecting a control and moving your cursor to the form, your mouse pointer will appear as crosshairs (it looks like a plus sign). You start at a location where you want your object to appear on the form and click your mouse. Now move your mouse with the mouse button depressed, and you will see the outline of your object. When you release the mouse, your object will appear.

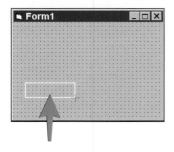

3 The Command Button

The Command Button is the control that can be associated with an action in the program. When the user clicks the command button at runtime, the code that is assigned to that button is executed.

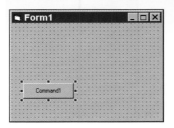

4 Choose the Object Properties

Once you have an object on your form, and that object is selected, the **Properties window** displays the properties for that object. The **Properties window** is where the appearance and characteristics of the object are set.

5 Add Additional Controls

You can add additional controls to your form. You may want to add the same control multiple times with different code or instructions behind each control.

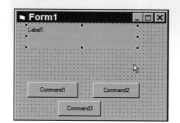

6 Additional Controls, Continued

Some controls are used to interact with a user, and have the user interact with the applications. Other controls or objects are for information or esthetics only. For example, you could use the Textbox object to add a name.

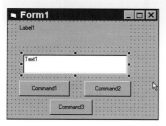

End

How-To Hints

Selecting Objects in the Toolbox

An alternate way of inserting objects into the form is to double-click an object. This will insert that object into the middle of the form and all you need to do is position it.

When you select an object from the **Toolbox** while keeping the control key depressed, you can add that object multiple times without having to re-select it.

How to Add Code to Your Form

So far, you have seen the ease with which you can generate the window display. Now you must examine how to assign the instructions that allow the objects to function. The code behind the objects gives directions for the application to follow. Each object has coded instructions associated with it.

Begin

1 Access the Code Window

The **Code window** can be accessed three different ways. Either select **Code** from the **View** menu, click the **View Code** button on the **Project Explorer** window, or double-click the object.

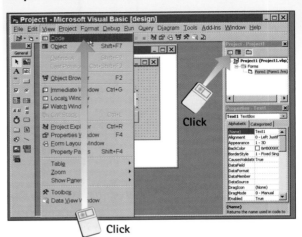

Click

Click

2 Enter Code in the Code Window

The **Code window**, which is actually a code editor, allows you to enter Visual Basic code for actions performed on an object. The drop-down lists at the top of the window list the objects on a form and their valid procedures. For example, a command button can have associated instructions—such as **keypress**, **gotfocus**, or **lostfocus**—that occur when it is clicked.

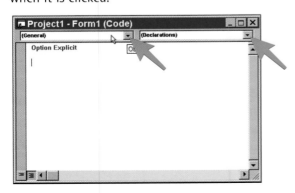

3 Event-Driven Procedure

When you select an object to assign code to, the **Code window** will automatically open up a **private sub** for the object name and its event (user action) that will trigger its execution.

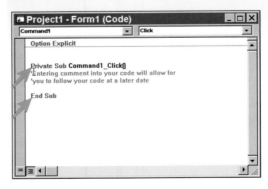

4 Comment Code

It is good programming practice to add comments to your procedures. This allows for someone to follow the logical flow or thought process when reviewing the code. Comments in Visual Basic are achieved by using a single quote. Notice that comments appear in a different color.

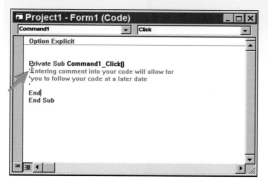

5 Enter Code

Now let's enter your first piece of code. For the **Click** event on the command1 button, you want to end the procedure. Let's type in **END** between the **SUB** statement and the **END SUB** statements.

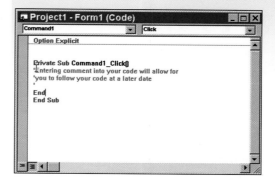

6 Return to the Form Screen

To return to the form screen, there are again three methods. Either press the **Shift** and **F7** keys, select **Object** from the **View** menu, or click the **View Object** button above the **Project Explorer** window.

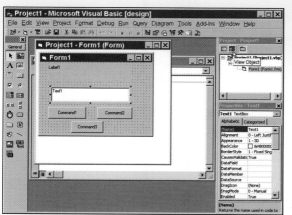

End

How to Use the MSGBOX Function

When you are coding, Visual Basic provides many built-in functions. A function is a predefined activity that will derive a standard result each time. One of the first basic functions your application needs is the ability to display messages to the user. This function is performed by way of the **MSGBOX** function or statement.

Begin

1 MSGBOX Usage

The **MSGBOX** is used to convey information and elicit a response from a user. The responses will guide the application in the direction of the user's choice.

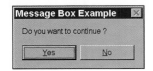

2 Messages and Warnings

The **MSGBOX** is used to display four types of messages—informational, warning, critical, and query. Depending on the type of message you want to display, the parameter of the function will change.

3 Follow the Format

As a built-in function, the **MSGBOX** has a format, or syntax, that must be followed. Syntax is the order in which the language expects the code to follow.

4 Choose Your Options

The different options will cause Visual Basic to generate different response possibilities. For example, you could use **VBWARNING**, **VBOKONLY**, or **VBYESNO**. For all available options, use the **Help** function.

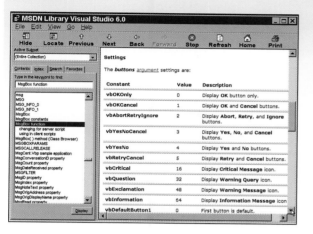

5 MSGBOX Variable

When you want to have **MSGBOX** determine the application direction or follow the user objectives, use a variable to store and test the user response. Variables will be discussed in greater detail later in the book.

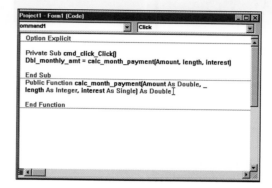

6 Control Application Flow

The **MSGBOX** is also used to determine the flow or direction that the user could take in the application, which can be determined by the buttons that appear on the **MSGBOX**.

End

How-To Hints

Format or Syntax

When you enter coding for a Visual Basic function, the syntax is displayed for you in a tip box.

How to Run Your Application

So far you have seen how to paint objects onto a form and put some coding behind your objects. Next you will see how to run, or execute, your application. Running your application during the development process allows you to see how your application will perform for the user.

Begin

1 Interactive Development

One of the major benefits of using Visual Basic as a development tool is the ability to run your application from the development environment during the development process.

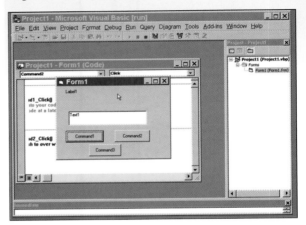

2 Run the Application

There are several ways to run or test your application. Either select the **Run** menu from the menu bar, press the **F5** key, or click the **Start** button on the **Toolbar**.

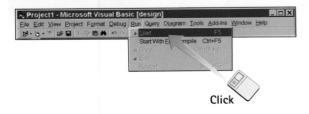

Click

3 Return to the Environment

After executing or running your application, you can return to your code by ending the application. This is accomplished by assigning the **END** instruction to a command button, or by clicking the **Close** button in the upper-right corner of the window.

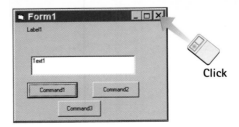

Click

4 Fix Any Errors

Error handling is discused later in this book; however, when you try to run the application, Visual Basic may give you an error message and highlight a line of code. This occurs because there is something wrong with the syntax of that line. You need to correct the line and continue.

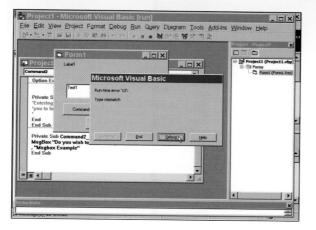

5 End Execution with an Error

In some cases, you may want to terminate the execution during an error message. The **End** button on the toolbar will accomplish this.

Click

6 Create an Executable Application

After you complete your application, you will be able to create an executable file. From the **File** menu, select **Make Project.EXE**. This will create an executable file for you.

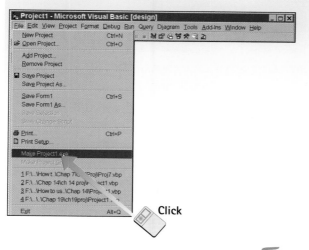

Click

End

Project

Let's review what you have learned in the this chapter. In this project, you will create your first Visual Basic application. You will incorporate several objects, and apply coding that will change the appearance of text. The goal of this project is to get you started using the elements within Visual Basic, and to develop your first applications.

1 Start a New Project

Let's start up Visual Basic and begin. Select the **Standard EXE** option from the **New** tab of the Visual Basic **New Project** screen.

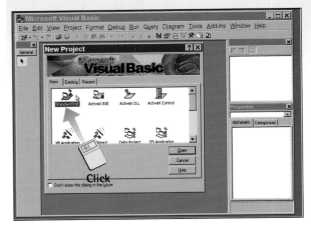

2 Add a Command Button

You will add three command buttons to your project. Each button accomplishs a separate task. Select the **Command Button** control icon from the **Toolbox**, and add it on **Form1**. This button will enable the user to change the default font of the text.

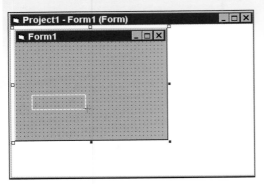

3 Add a Second Command Button

Now let's add a second command button to the right of the first command button. This button will change the text back to its original or default values.

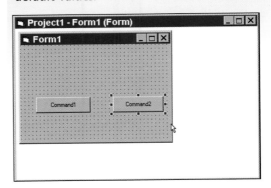

4 Add the Final Command Button

Let add a third command button. This command button will function as the Exit button and will terminate your application.

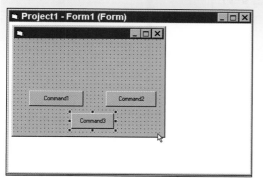

5 Add a Label

Select the **Label** control icon from the **Toolbox** and add a label to the top of the form. This label will be used to display text on the form itself.

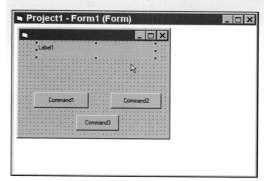

6 Add a Textbox

Double-click the **TextBox** control icon in the **Toolbox**, and position it under the label on the form. The textbox will contain text.

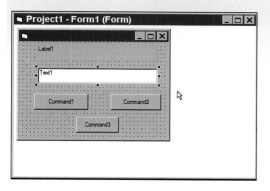

7 Add Some Code

Let's add some code. Click the **View Code** button. The code that you are adding are instructions that will be executed when an event is triggered.

Click

Continues

Project Continued

8 Select Form Load

From the drop-down listbox on the left of the form, select **Form Load**. Notice that there are two drop-down lists. The list on the left contains the valid objects on the form. The list on the right holds all the valid events.

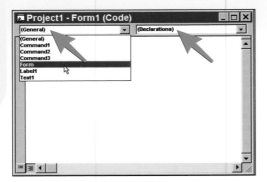

9 See the Code Editor in Action

Between the **Private Sub** and **End Sub** type in **Form1.** your different options appear. After the code text **form1.**, you will be presented with a list of valid options. These options represent actions that are to be applied to the object.

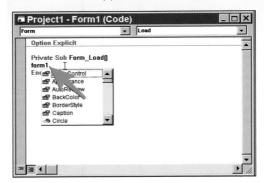

10 Enter Form Load Code

Enter the following code (shown in the figure) for **Form_Load()**. Here, you enter the code or actions for when the form is loaded.

11 Enter the Command1 Event Code

For **Command1_click()**, enter the following code (shown in the figure), which will display a **MSGBOX** and allow the user to change the font in the textbox.

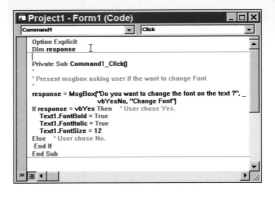

12 Enter the Command2 Event Code

Select **Command2_click()** and enter the following code (shown in the figure). Here you will use the **MSGBOX** as an informational message and change the font back to its original format.

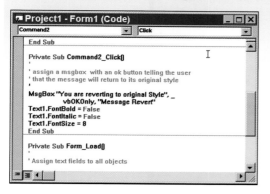

13 Enter the Command3 Event Code

Assign the **End** command to **Command3_click()**; this is the command that will end the running of your application.

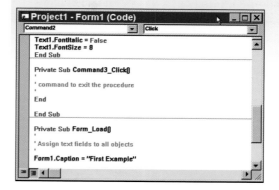

14 Save Your Work

To save your work, select the **Save Project** button on the **Toolbar**. Saving your work often is a good practice.

15 Save the Form

Create a new folder by clicking the **Create New Folder** icon, and **Save** your form in the new folder.

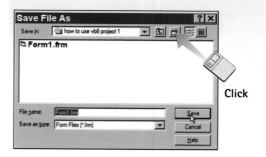

Click

Continues

Project Continued

16 Save Your Project

Now, **Save** your project in the same new folder. Remember that each form, module, and project are saved separately.

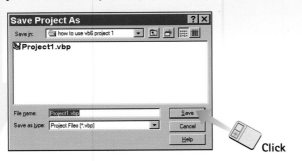

Click

17 Run the Application

Select the **Start** icon from the **Toolbar** and start your application.

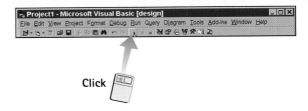

Click

18 Change the Font Command

Now it's time to test your application. Click the **Change Fonts** button, click **Yes** in the **MSG-BOX**, and observe the **MSGBOX** in action. Verify that the font of the textbox has changed. You have just executed the code in the **Click** event of the **Command1** button.

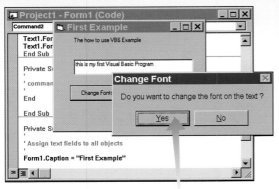

Click

19 Test the Default Command

Click the **Default** command button. Again, when you click the **Default** button, you are triggering the **Click** event of **Command2**, causing the code for **Command2_click** to execute.

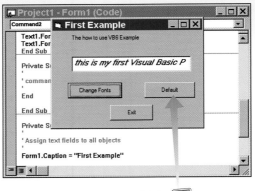

Click

20 Watch MSGBOX in Action

Click the **OK MSGBOX** button. Once again, notice that the code or commands entered for the **MSGBOX** were executed.

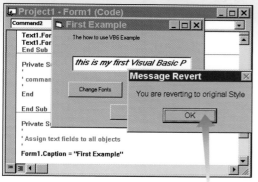

Click

21 Exit the Application

Now click the **Exit** command button and return to your development environment.

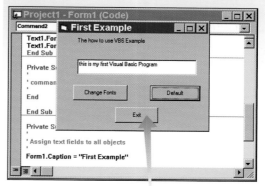

Click

22 Create an Executable

Now, let's create an EXE which can run on its own. Click the **File** menu and select **Make Project1.EXE** to create an executable file.

Find the folder where you saved your form and project. Save the EXE file in that folder.

Click

23 Test Your First Executable Project

Find the EXE file and double-click it.

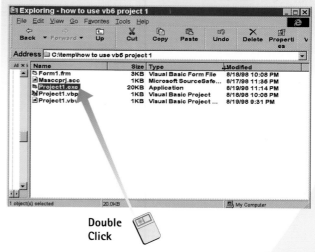

Double Click

End

Task

4

Enhancing the Project

*W*hat you have seen so far is what Visual Basic is, and some of the basic aspects and attributes of an application. Here you will examine how to enhance your application. You will learn how to add additional screens and colors, and how to change fonts. You will also discover methods and properties of forms and controls that will jazz up your application. Also covered in this chapter are some of the **Code Editor** features and how to use them. ●

TASK *1*

How to Add a Form

Most applications will require several forms. You could have an application that requires multiple forms—some which you could consider standard. In fact, Visual Basic provides several predefined forms that can be added to your application, such as a logon, an About, or a splash screen. Each form that is added to an application will be saved as a separate file with a .FRM extension. All forms can be viewed and accessed from the **Project Explorer** window.

Begin

1 Add a New Form

To add a new form to an existing application, you can select **Add Form** from the **Project** menu, or use the **Form** button on the **Toolbar**.

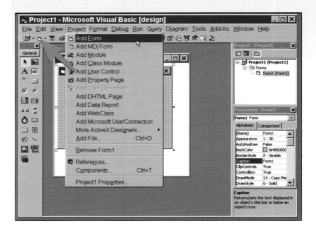

2 Using the Add Form Dialog Box

After you select **Add Form** from the **Project** menu, the **Add Form** dialog box allows you to add a blank form. It also allows you to select some predefined screens.

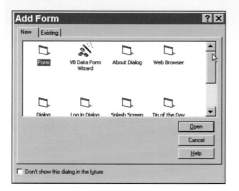

3 Using the Login Screen

The login screen will generate a generic screen, which asks for a **User Name** and **Password**. The screen can be changed to your requirements, and the code needs to be modified.

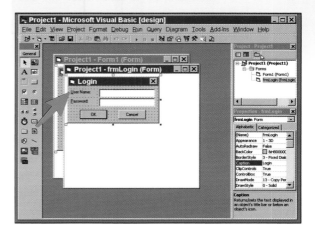

4 Using the About Box

The About box form, which is available in most window applications under Help, displays application information. The version and release numbers are shown, as well as the registration information about the product.

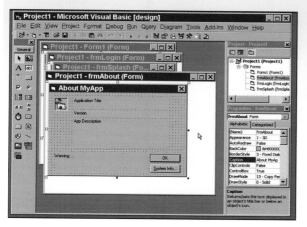

5 Using the Splash Screen

The splash screen is also a predefined form that is used by applications at startup. In fact, the first screen you see when you start Visual Basic is a splash screen.

End

How-To Hints

Splash Form

It was previously explained that in the **Project Properties** you could select your startup object. The **Splash Form** should not be selected as a startup object, but rather have code display your splash screen. You can then hide the splash screen, when your application loads.

How to Create App Objects

An **App** object is a global or application-wide object. Using the **App** keyword, you can extract and use information about the application, such as **Title**, **Version**, or **Company Name** (this information is maintained in the **Project Properties** of your application). Some of these objects are used in the **About** and **Splash Forms**.

Begin

1 Display the Title

The title of your application can be displayed in the border of a form. Setting the **Caption** property to the **App.title** will accomplish this.

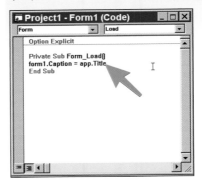

2 Create the Version Number

A product version usually relates to three different types of releases—major, minor, and revision. You have access to the version number in the **Project** menu, as three distinct fields. These three fields can be concatenated to display the release version.

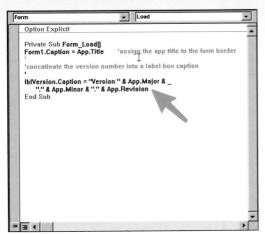

3 Create a Path

The **App.path** information will return the directory where the application is stored. This is useful information if you need to create or retrieve data files that are stored in the same directory.

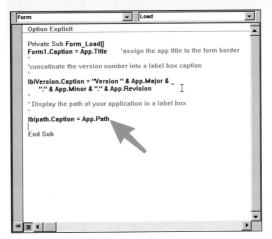

4 Create the Copyright Information

The copyright information will display any legal licensing requirements that you enter in the project properties. This information is displayed in the About screen.

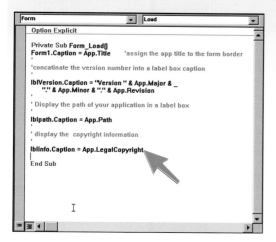

```
Form                          Load
  Option Explicit

  Private Sub Form_Load()
  Form1.Caption = App.Title        'assign the app title to the form border
  '
  'concatinate the version number into a label box caption
  '
  lblVersion.Caption = "Version " & App.Major & _
       "." & App.Minor & "." & App.Revision
  '
  ' Display the path of your application in a label box
  '
  lblpath.Caption = App.Path
  '
  ' display the  copyright information
  '
  lblinfo.Caption = App.LegalCopyright
  '
  End Sub
```

5 Display a Project File Description

The Project file description, which is also entered in the **Project Properties**, is information that can be displayed in help screens.

```
Form                          Load
  Option Explicit

  Private Sub Form_Load()
  'set the file description
  Label1.Caption = App.fil
  End Sub          FileDescription
                   HelpFile
                   hInstance
                   LegalCopyright
                   LegalTrademarks
                   LogEvent
                   LogMode
```

6 Display More Descriptions

The **Project Properties** allow you to keep general information about the project, as well as specific information about your application. Most of the information can be retrieved using the **App** method—you can even include your company's name.

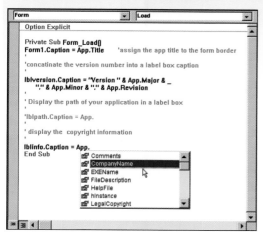

```
Form                          Load
  Option Explicit

  Private Sub Form_Load()
  Form1.Caption = App.Title        'assign the app title to the form border
  '
  'concatinate the version number into a label box caption
  '
  lblversion.Caption = "Version " & App.Major & _
       "." & App.Minor & "." & App.Revision
  '
  ' Display the path of your application in a label box
  '
  'lblpath.Caption = App.
  '
  ' display the  copyright information
  '
  lblinfo.Caption = App.
  End Sub          Comments
                   CompanyName
                   EXEName
                   FileDescription
                   HelpFile
                   hInstance
                   LegalCopyright
```

End

How to Use the Inputbox Function

A requirement in most programming languages is the capability to prompt or get information from a user. In Visual Basic, there are several ways to obtain information from a user. The easiest way is to add a predefined dialog box or function to your application. The **Inputbox**, a function similar to the **MSGBOX** function, provides that capability.

Begin

1 Learn the Syntax

Just as with any built-in functions, the **Inputbox** has a required syntax. The **Inputbox** function displays the OK and Cancel buttons.

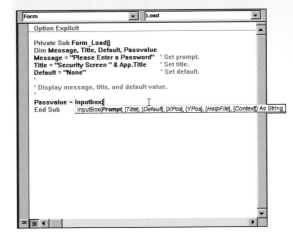

2 Set the Prompt

The first argument or required field of the **Inputbox** is the prompt. This string is the text that will be displayed as the question.

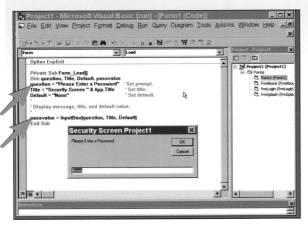

3 Review the Answer

When you prompt a user for information, you must have the ability to review and work with the user's response. You therefore store the response in a variable.

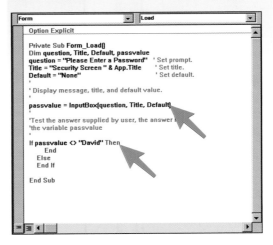

4 Enter the Default Answer

The default value is the value assigned to the variable if the user does not enter a response.

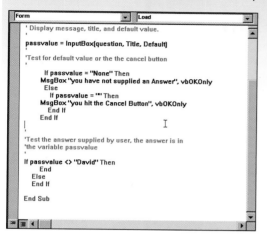

```
Form                    ▼   Load              ▼

' Display message, title, and default value.

passvalue = InputBox(question, Title, Default)

'Test for default value or the the cancel button
'
        If passvalue = "None" Then
        MsgBox "you have not supplied an Answer", vbOKOnly
        Else
            If passvalue = "" Then
        MsgBox "you hit the Cancel Button", vbOKOnly
            End If
        End If
                                    I

'Test the answer supplied by user, the answer is in
'the variable passvalue
'
If passvalue <> "David" Then
        End
        Else
        End If

End Sub
```

5 Test for Variable Value

Your code should test for a valid response from the user. If you are prompting for a numeric value to apply to an arithmetic expression, you need to validate that a number was supplied as opposed to a letter.

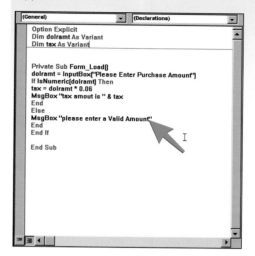

```
(General)                ▼   (Declarations)         ▼

Option Explicit
Dim dolramt As Variant
Dim tax As Variant


Private Sub Form_Load()
dolramt = InputBox("Please Enter Purchase Amount")
If IsNumeric(dolramt) Then
tax = dolramt * 0.06
MsgBox "tax amout is " & tax
End
Else
MsgBox "please enter a Valid Amount"
End
End If                           I

End Sub
```

6 Using the Variable

After validation has been preformed on the variable, it is available to use in the code.

```
Form                    ▼   Load              ▼

' Display message, title, and default value.

passvalue = InputBox(question, Title, Default)

'Test for default value or the the cancel button
'
        If passvalue = "None" Then
        MsgBox "you have not supplied an Answer", vbOKOnly
        Else
            If passvalue = "" Then
        MsgBox "you hit the Cancel Button", vbOKOnly
            End If
        End If
                                    I

'Test the answer supplied by user, the answer is in
'the variable passvalue
'
If passvalue <> "David" Then
        End
        Else
        End If

End Sub
```

End

How to Use Properties

A property is data about an object or a form. They define the characteristics of an object such as size, color, and position. Property values can be viewed and changed in the **Properties window**. Typing over the existing value can change some properties—such as **Name** or **Caption**—while other properties, including **Font** and **Color**, are changed using a drop-down list box. To work with the properties of an object, that item must be in focus, or selected.

Begin

1 Learn the Naming Conventions

It is good programming practice and a Microsoft recommendation that objects have a standard naming convention—a three-letter prefix that identifies the object, followed by a descriptive name. For example, if you name a command button **cmdEXIT**, it becomes clear from the name that the object is a command button intended to exit the application.

2 Add a Form Caption

The form's **Caption** property is the text that appears on the border of a form. As you are typing the change, you will notice that the border title is changing.

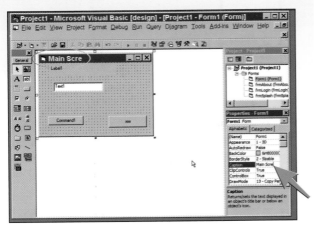

3 Tweak the Caption

Similarly, when you change the caption for a command button, the text that appears on the command button changes. With the Command Button control, you can create keyboard strokes to execute the command. If you enter an ampersand (&) prior to a letter, that letter will have an underscore and can be executed by pressing **Alt** plus the letter.

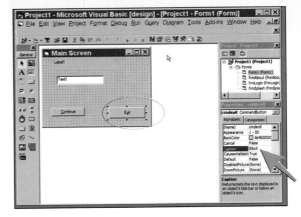

4 Change the Font

When you select the **Font** property in the **Properties window**, you will see a little box to the right side. When you click that selection box, the **Font** dialog box opens, giving you a choice of fonts and sizes to choose from.

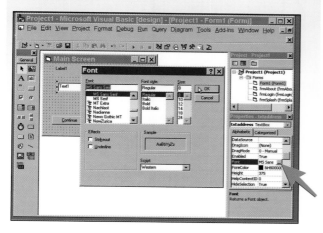

5 Select a Color

When you click the **BackColor** property in the **Properties window**, you will see a drop-down arrow. Click the arrow and select the **Palette** tab to select your desired color.

End

How-To Hints

Naming Convention

When objects have a clear naming convention, your job in the **Code window** becomes easier, because the object names in the drop-down list will have descriptive names.

Watch Out!

Object properties can be changed or defined in the code, as you saw in your first project when you changed the command button caption.

How to Use More Properties

Although the most commonly used properties are **Name**, **Caption**, and **Font**, there are several others that are important and worth discussing. These additional properties are useful during program execution.

1 Using the Enable Property

The **Enable** property, which has a **True** or **False** value, allows you to enable or disable an object. As an example, if you display a screen where you're prompted for a password, you may want to disable the **Continue** button until the password is populated.

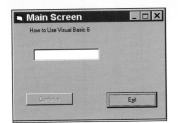

2 Using the Text Property

The **Text** property is for a textbox, and allows you to change the text that appears in the textbox. This value is usually left blank for data input or display.

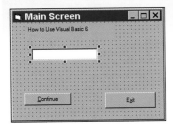

3 Using the ToolTip Property

The **ToolTip** property allows you to enter a tip. When your application is running and your user allows the cursor to rest over an object, the tip will be displayed.

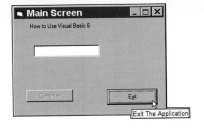

4 Using the TabIndex Property

When a window application is running and the user presses the **Tab** key, control usually changes to the next object. The **TabIndex** property enables you to determine the tab order of your objects.

5 Using the BorderStyle Property

The **BorderStyle** property defines the look and usability of the form. You can allow the user full access to the movement, maximize, and minimize options of a form. Or, for no movement at all, you can define a form in which the user will have no controls.

6 Learning the Properties Window

When you click a property item, there is a message area under the **Properties window** that explains what effect the property has on its object.

End

How to Use Methods

Just as Visual Basic has predefined functions that generate objects like **MSGBOX** or **Inputbox**, it also has predefined methods for objects. Methods are actions that are applied to objects. These are not to be confused with properties, which are the attributes of an object or a form. The methods are the operations that objects follow.

Begin

1 Display the Form

To have your application move from one screen to another, you use the **Show** method. This method, which is entered into the code, will display the form.

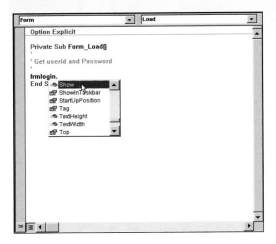

2 Remove the Form

Again, you use another method to remove a form from view. When a user has completed work on a form and you want to remove a form, you use the **Hide** method.

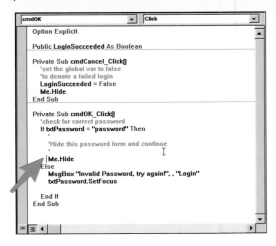

3 Print

The **PrintForm** method can be used to print out forms or reports to your printer. The **PrintForm** method will also send text or graphics to your printer.

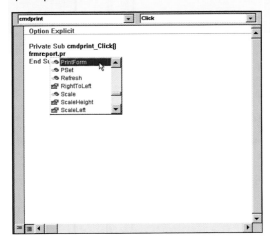

4 Using the Move Method

Although properties and methods are different, in some cases they accomplish the same result. The **Move** method can be achieved by setting the position (top and left) properties.

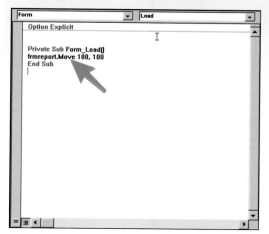

```
Form                          Load
Option Explicit

Private Sub Form_Load()
frmreport.Move 100, 100
End Sub
```

5 Using the SetFocus Method

The **SetFocus** method allows you to set the focus to a particular object. You can see its use in the logon screen. When a user enters an invalid password, an error message will appear and the user will be back at the password textbox.

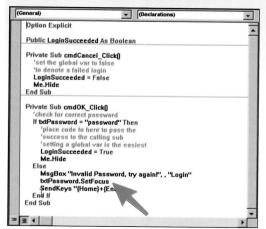

```
(General)                     (Declarations)
Option Explicit

Public LoginSucceeded As Boolean

Private Sub cmdCancel_Click()
    'set the global var to false
    'to denote a failed login
    LoginSucceeded = False
    Me.Hide
End Sub

Private Sub cmdOK_Click()
    'check for correct password
    If txtPassword = "password" Then
        'place code to here to pass the
        'success to the calling sub
        'setting a global var is the easiest
        LoginSucceeded = True
        Me.Hide
    Else
        MsgBox "Invalid Password, try again!", , "Login"
        txtPassword.SetFocus
        SendKeys "{Home}+{En
    End If
End Sub
```

End

Using the Code Editor

When you are entering code into the **Code Editor**, you have the same capabilities as you do with other editors, such as cut and paste. However, Visual Basic provides you with an interactive code editor. This means that as you type in functions or methods, Visual Basic displays the correct syntax for the statement. It also provides some error checking as you move on to the next line.

Begin

1 Add Comments

When you add comments to your code, the **Code Editor** displays these lines in a different color. Visual Basic values will also appear in a different color. This allows you to review your code in an extremely easy way.

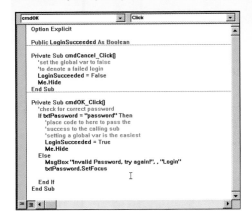

2 Change Methods and Properties

When you change the properties or methods of an object in the **Code Editor**, the valid available options appear after you type the dot. This allows you to determine what options are available and also identify typing mistakes when the list does not appear.

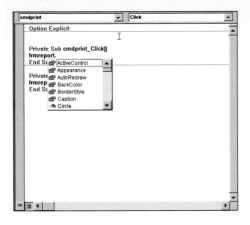

3 Call up the Function's Syntax

Just as the valid options appear for properties and methods, the syntax appears when you are entering a function like the **MSGBOX**.

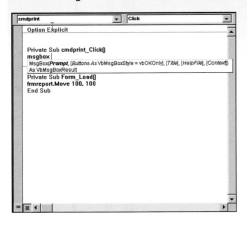

4 Handling Errors

In some cases when you are entering code, the **Code Editor** will determine that there is an error and will display an error message.

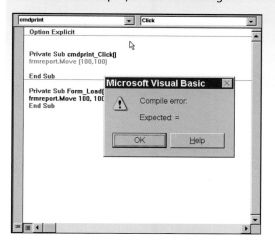

5 Handling Runtime Errors

The **Code Editor** will also display errors that are caught at runtime. It highlights the section and line with the error.

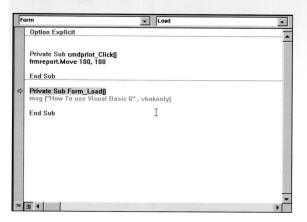

6 Tab Your Code

Another nice feature of the **Code Editor** is how the tabs are handled. When you indent your code with the **Tab** key, and press **Enter** to go to the next line, the next line will align in the tabbed order.

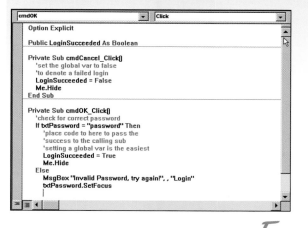

End

How-To Hints

Code Continuation

In order to make your code easier to read and follow, you may want to continue commands in two lines. To inform Visual Basic that a line is continuing, you use an underscore (_) at the end of the line.

Task

5

Changing the Project's Interface

*T*he simplest of Visual Basic applications consists of a single form that contains one or more controls. This allows the user to interact with it to perform some type of action or function. However, as you start to add more functions to the application, you must provide the user with a way of selecting them. An application can contain many different forms that perform specific functions or actions. In addition, an application can come in three separate types—the Multiple Document Interface (MDI), the Single Document Interface (SDI), and the Explorer Interface. Each of these types can be found in Windows. The **Windows Explorer** uses the Explorer Interface, whereas Microsoft Word uses the Multiple Document Interface, and Notepad uses the Single Document Interface.

In this chapter, you are going to learn how to work with a single form while adding two of the most common methods of providing the user with choices—the **Form** menu and toolbars. In addition, you will also see how to add an About form to the project that will display information about the application itself. ●

How to Include a Menu

Menus are one of the easiest objects to add to a Visual Basic application—not because there is a **Menu Editor**, but because menus are simple to work with. Once the menu options are defined, you can use them the same way you would use a command button. However, menus allow you to group or nest liked functions together. To work with menus, you must first add them to the form where they are needed.

Begin

1 Display the Form

You cannot just add a menu; you must first display the form you want the menu on by selecting the form in the **Project Explorer** window and clicking the **View Object** button.

Click

2 Open the Menu Editor

After you have the form displayed on the screen, you can open the **Menu Editor** by clicking the **Menu Editor** button on the Visual Basic **Toolbar**, or by right-clicking the form and choosing **Menu Editor** from the pop-up menu.

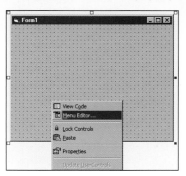

3 Add a Menu Option

The **Menu Editor** provides you with several options that you can set for each menu option that you add. To add a new menu option, you must enter a **Caption** and a **Name** for the option.

4 Add Multiple Levels to the Menu

If every menu option that you add were at the same level, the menu would quickly become unusable. To group different functions together, you can add menu options at different levels using the right and left arrows in the **Menu Editor**. Indenting an option to the right makes it a choice of the option above it.

5 Include Menu Shortcut Keys

In most applications, you have some way of accessing the menu options without using the mouse. This is done by using shortcut keys. They can be assigned to a menu option using the **Shortcut** drop-down list to select the key sequence that you want.

6 Finish the Process

Once you have added all of the required menu options, click the **OK** button to close the **Menu Editor**. You will then see the new menu you have created displayed on the form.

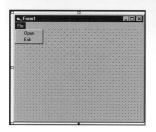

7 Add Code to a Menu Option

To add code to a menu option, click that menu option to display the **Code Editor** for that option's **Click** event. Then add the required code to that event.

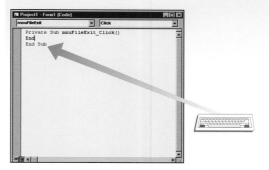

End

How-To Hints

Disabling a Menu Item

There are times that you want a menu item to be disabled. You can do this at design time by un-checking the **Enabled** checkbox for a given menu option. Then at runtime, you could change the property to **True** to enable it for use.

Adding a Checkmark

In some applications, a menu option is used to specify a setting a some type. Using the **Checked** property of the menu option would display a check next to the menu option when it is being used.

2

How to Use Toolbars in the Project

A second method of providing choices is to use the Toolbar control in your application. Toolbars are a lot like menus, except that they normally use pictures or images and buttons instead of words. You can even give the user the ability to add and remove buttons on the **Toolbar** to customize it to their liking.

Begin

1 Using Pictures Instead of Words

Toolbars give the user an image of the function instead of words. Most Windows applications use a standard set of images for common functions.

2 Allow the User to Customize

Allowing the user to customize the **Toolbar** gives him control over the buttons that are displayed. Using this feature is as simple as double-clicking the **Toolbar** to display the **Customize Toolbar** dialog.

3 Add the Toolbar Control

To use the Toolbar control, you must add the **Microsoft Windows Common Controls 6.0** option to the project using the **Components** dialog, which is displayed by choosing **Project**, **Components** from the Visual Basic menu.

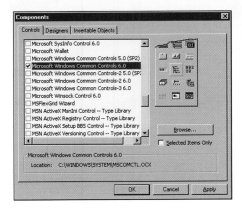

4 Place a Toolbar on a Form

A toolbar is placed on a form the same way as any other control—just double-click the **Toolbar** control button. However, it can be placed only on the top or bottom of the form.

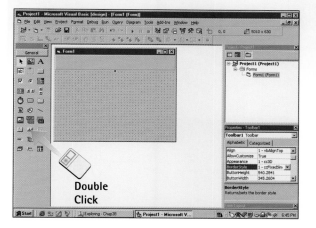

Double Click

5 Place ImageLists on the Form

In order to have images displayed in the toolbar buttons, you must have at least one ImageList control on the same form as the toolbar. The ImageList control is contained in the Windows Common Control that you have already added to your project—simply double-click the **ImageList** button in the **Toolbox**.

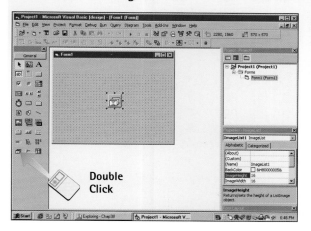

Double Click

6 Add a Picture to the Image List

Before adding buttons to the **Toolbar**, add the images you want to use to the ImageList control by clicking the **Insert Picture** button on the picture in the ImageList **Property Pages**.

7 Connect the ImageList Control

To access the images on the **Toolbar**, you need to set the **ImageList** property to the name of the ImageList control you placed on the form.

End

How-To Hints

Using Common Pictures

Visual Basic 6 comes with many common images that you can use on the **Toolbar** that are very familiar to you and anyone else who has used a Windows application before. They can be found in the Program Files\Microsoft Visual Studio\Common\Graphics directory on your computer.

How to Add Buttons to the Toolbar

Placing a toolbar on a form is only the first of three steps in the process of adding toolbars to your application. The second step is to actually add the buttons you want to the **Toolbar**. In addition, in Visual Basic 6, you can add a menu-like drop-down list to a button.

Begin

1 Display the Properties Dialog

To insert buttons, you must display the **Toolbar**'s **Property Pages** by right-clicking on the toolbar and choosing **Properties** from the pop-up menu.

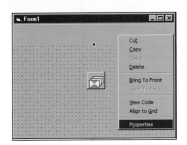

2 Insert a Button

The **Buttons** tab provides you with everything you need to add buttons to the **Toolbar**. To add a button, click the **Insert Button** command button and then fill in the required properties.

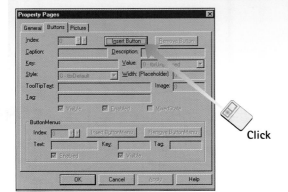

Click

3 Define a Button Key

For each button that you add to the **Toolbar**, you should define a **Key** string that will be used later to identify that button in the program code.

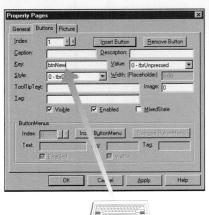

4 Assign an Image

After adding a button, assign an image to it by entering the **Image** key you entered for that button image.

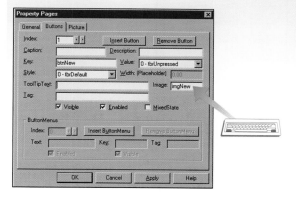

5 Add ToolTips

Another feature that you can add to a button is **ToolTip Text**, which is displayed if the mouse is placed on the button.

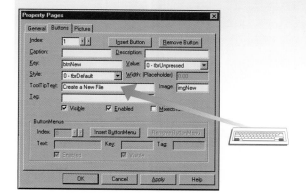

6 Choose a Button Style

The button's **Style** property lets you specify how the button will appear to the user. For most buttons, you will add the default style that should be used.

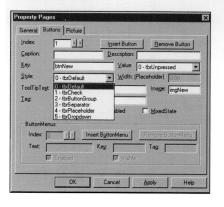

7 Add a Button Drop-Down Menu

One of the button styles allows you to add a menu to the button that is displayed as a drop-down list. Each menu item is added at the bottom of the **Buttons** tab in the **ButtonMenus** area.

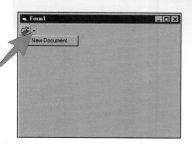

End

How-To Hints

Why Use Button Menus?

Button menus let you provide the same grouping of functions or options that the **Menu bar** does by assigning them to a single button on the **Toolbar**.

TASK 4

How to Add Code to the Toolbar

Adding code to enable the buttons on the **Toolbar** is the third and final step in adding a toolbar to the application. Using the **Code Editor**, you add code the same way as any other control on the form. The **Toolbar** events actually provide a variable that helps you identify which button was clicked.

Begin

1 The ButtonClick Event

The most important event for the **Toolbar** is the **ButtonClick** event. This is the event that is executed when the user clicks a button on the **Toolbar**.

2 Using the Select Statement

The **Select** statement is used in conjunction with the **Button** variable in the event and the **Key** strings that you assigned for each button. This allows you to know which button was actually clicked.

3 The ButtonMenuClick Event

If you are using the button menus, you will also need to know when a menu item was clicked and which item it was. The **ButtonMenuClick** event does this for you the same way the **ButtonClick** event works for buttons.

4 The ButtonDropDown Event

Sometimes you will need to know when a button menu is displayed. This is done by using the **ButtonDropDown** event, which is executed whenever a button menu list is displayed.

5 Using Button Groups

Button groups provide a way for the user to select one option from a set of options on the **Toolbar**. Button groups can be seen when used for text alignment, but they can be used with any type of selection. Creating button groups is done by adding a group of buttons to the **Toolbar** and setting the **Style** property for each of them to **tbrButtonGroup**.

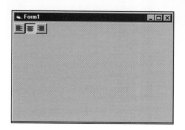

End

How-To Hints

Using Button Keys

Buttons keys make it easier for you to read the code you have written for the **Toolbar**. Button keys allow you to check for a button by a name instead of by a number.

Initializing the Button Group

Most button groups have a default setting that needs to be initialized as the form is displayed. This is done by setting the **Value** property of the default button in the group to **tbrPressed**. This will force that button to be pressed when displayed. The user can then change the selection by clicking the required button.

How to Add an About Form

Most applications have an About dialog that is displayed from the **Help** menu list. This form generally displays information about the application using the **App** object. The information displayed by the **App** object is assigned by you in the **Project Properties** dialog box.

Begin

1 Using an About Form

An About dialog can be used to display almost any type of information. However, the common information is about the version and licensing of the application.

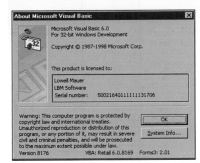

2 Add the About Form

While you can create an About dialog from scratch, it is far easier to use the About form template that comes with Visual Basic. By right-clicking the **Project Explorer** window and choosing **Add Form**, the **Add Form** dialog is displayed showing all of the different templates that can be added to the project. Select the **About Dialog** and click **OK**.

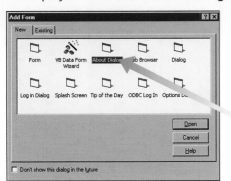

Click

3 Add the About Menu Option

The About dialog is usually displayed by adding a Help option to the menu and then adding an About... item to the Help menu.

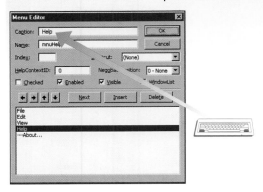

4 Display the About Form

The About dialog is then displayed by the **Show** method when that menu item is clicked.

```
mnuHelpAbout        Click

Private Sub mnuHelpAbout_Click()
frmAbout.Show
End Sub
```

5 Using the App Object

The **App** object can be used to display the information that you have entered into the **Project Properties** dialog box. By using this object, you can initialize the different labels that are already on the form.

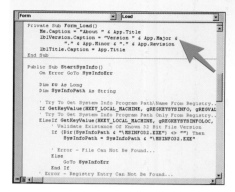

```
Form        Load

Private Sub Form_Load()
    Me.Caption = "About " & App.Title
    lblVersion.Caption = "Version " & App.Major &
        "." & App.Minor & "." & App.Revision
    lblTitle.Caption = App.Title
End Sub

Public Sub StartSysInfo()
    On Error GoTo SysInfoErr

    Dim rc As Long
    Dim SysInfoPath As String

    ' Try To Get System Info Program Path\Name From Registry..
    If GetKeyValue(HKEY_LOCAL_MACHINE, gREGKEYSYSINFO, gREGVAL
    ' Try To Get System Info Program Path Only From Registry..
    ElseIf GetKeyValue(HKEY_LOCAL_MACHINE, gREGKEYSYSINFOLOC,
        ' Validate Existance Of Known 32 Bit File Version
        If (Dir(SysInfoPath & "\MSINFO32.EXE") <> "") Then
            SysInfoPath = SysInfoPath & "\MSINFO32.EXE"

        ' Error - File Can Not Be Found...
        Else
            GoTo SysInfoErr
        End If
    ' Error - Registry Entry Can Not Be Found...
```

6 Set the Information Manually

If you do not want to use the **App** object to display the information, or the information you want in the About dialog is very customized, you can assign the information yourself.

```
Form        Load

Private Sub Form_Load()
    Me.Caption = "About " & App.Title
    lblVersion.Caption = "Version " & App.Major & _
        "." & App.Minor & "." & App.Revision
    lblTitle.Caption = App.Title
    lblDisclaimer.caption = "This program is protected!"
End Sub

Public Sub StartSysInfo()
    On Error GoTo SysInfoErr

    Dim rc As Long
    Dim SysInfoPath As String

    ' Try To Get System Info Program Path\Name From Registry..
    If GetKeyValue(HKEY_LOCAL_MACHINE, gREGKEYSYSINFO, gREGVAL
    ' Try To Get System Info Program Path Only From Registry..
    ElseIf GetKeyValue(HKEY_LOCAL_MACHINE, gREGKEYSYSINFOLOC,
        ' Validate Existance Of Known 32 Bit File Version
        If (Dir(SysInfoPath & "\MSINFO32.EXE") <> "") Then
            SysInfoPath = SysInfoPath & "\MSINFO32.EXE"

        ' Error - File Can Not Be Found...
        Else
            GoTo SysInfoErr
        End If
```

7 Add a Picture to the Form

On the About form template is an Image control which you can use to display the picture that you want to associate with the application. Changing the **Picture** property of the Image control will display the selected picture.

End

How-To Hints

System Info and Additional Info

Using an About box allows you to display information about you or your company by adding a command button to display an additional form in the application only from the About box.

Project

Creating an application that is easy to use means that you will try to make use of some common elements that can be found in almost any Windows application. This means adding menus and toolbars to your application. If you look at any Windows application, there are usually several menus and tool buttons that are the same. This project will step you through the process of adding the most common of elements of the menu and toolbar.

1 Start a New Project

In Visual Basic, pull down the **File** menu and choose **New Project**. This will display the **New Project** dialog box.

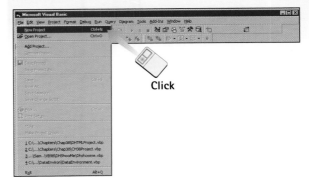

Click

2 Select the Standard EXE Project

Select the **Standard EXE** from the **New Project** dialog box and click the **OK** button.

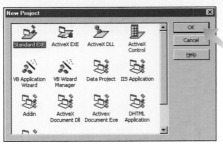

Click

3 Display the Components Dialog

Pull down the **Project** menu and choose **Components**. This will display the **Components** dialog, which is used to add additional controls to the project.

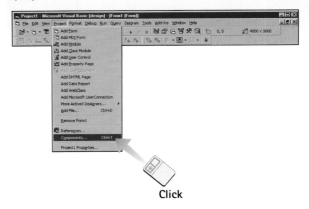

Click

4 Add the Windows Controls

Now find the **Microsoft Windows Common Controls 6.0** entry in the list and click the checkbox to select it. Then click **OK** to add it to the project.

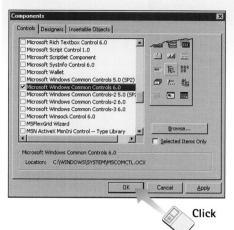

Click

5 Place the Toolbar

Double-click the **Toolbar** control button in the **Toolbox** to add the **Toolbar** to the form.

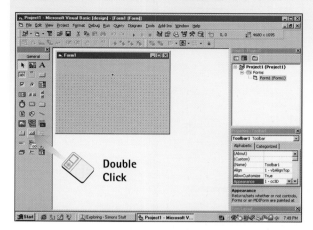

Double Click

6 Add an ImageList Control

Double-click the **ImageList** control button in the **Toolbox** to add it to the form.

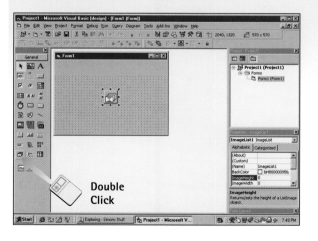

Double Click

7 Display the Menu Editor

With the default form displayed, click the **Menu Editor** button on the Visual Basic **Toolbar**.

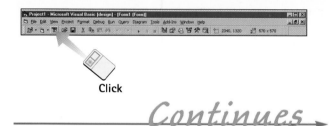

Click

Continues

8 Add the Top-Level Menu Items

Add the following items (File, Edit, View, Window, Help) as shown using the File item as the example.

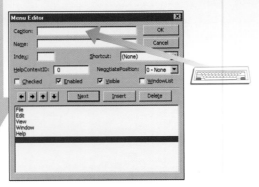

9 Add the File Menu Subitems

For the File menu, add the following items to its second level (New, Open, Close, Save, Exit) as shown.

10 Add the Edit Menu Subitems

For the Edit menu, add the following items to its second level (Cut, Copy, Paste, Delete) as shown.

11 Add the Window Menu Subitems

For the Window menu, add the following items to its second level (Tile Horizontally, Tile Vertically, Cascade, Arrange Icons) as shown.

12 Add the Help Menu Subitems

For the Help menu, add the following item to its second level (About the Project) as shown.

13 Display the ImageList Control

Right-click the ImageList control, choose **Properties**, and select the **Images** tab.

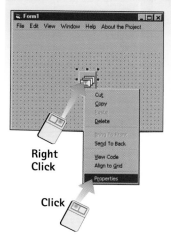

14 Add Pictures to the ImageList

Using the **Insert Picture** button, add the **Images** to the ImageList control.

15 Display the Toolbar Properties

Right-click the **Toolbar**, choose **Properties**, and then click the **Buttons** tab.

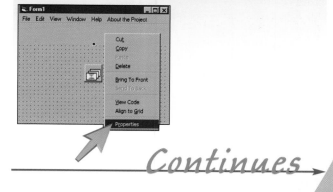

Continues

16 Attach the ImageList

Display the **Toolbar Property Pages** and select the image list you want to use from the **ImageList** property drop-down list.

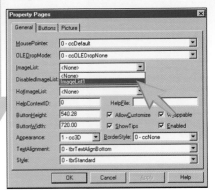

17 Adding the New Button

Click **Insert Button** again and enter the **Key** and **ToolTip Text** for the New button as shown.

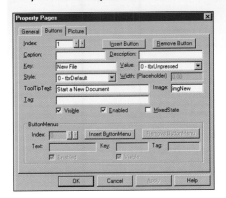

18 Adding the Exit Button

Click **Insert Button** again and enter the **Key** and **ToolTip Text** for the Exit button as shown.

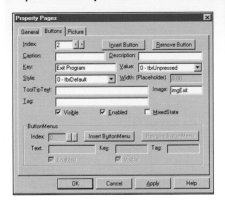

19 Enable the Toolbar with Code

Double-click the **Toolbar** to display its **Click** event routine in the **Code Editor**. Then enter the code shown that will display which button was clicked using a **MSGBOX** statement.

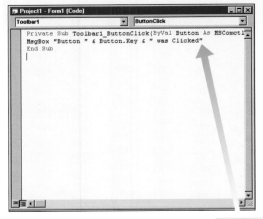

20 Add Code to a Menu Option

Pull down the **File** menu and choose **Open**. This will display the **Click** event for the Open menu option in the **Code Editor**. Enter the line of code shown to display a **MSGBOX**.

21 Exit the Program from the Menu

Pull down the **File** menu and choose **Exit**. This will display the **Click** event for the Exit menu option in the **Code Editor**. Enter the **END** statement which will end the execution of the program.

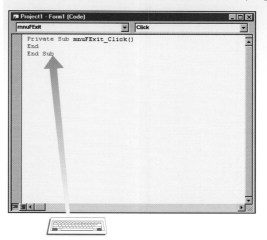

22 Exit from the Toolbar

Double-click the **Toolbar** to display the **Click** event in the **Code Editor**. Then enter the code shown to exit the program when the Exit button is clicked.

End

Task

6

Using the Basic Language

*A*pplication development requires your programming language to display screens, show information, accept input, and perform data manipulation. This consists of calculations to numeric data, as well as the ability to review, compare, and change string data. You have reviewed how to display screens and also accept information. This section examines how to create valid expressions, which perform arithmetic calculations and string manipulation. You will work with functions such as date and time. You also review what variables are and how to define and use them properly. ●

How to Define Variables

Most, if not all, programming languages have the capability of storing temporary information. This information is data that is needed by your programs while your application is running. Visual Basic provides variables and constants as a mechanism of storing such information. A variable is simply a reserved and named location in memory where you can store and recall information when needed. It is similar to a calculator, where you can store a number in memory and then recall it as desired. This task examines how to define and use these variables.

Begin

1 Using the Dim Statement

The **Dim**, or Dimension, statement will reserve a location in memory and assign a name to that location. When you use this statement, you are requesting Visual Basic to save an area in memory where information can be stored or retrieved by using the dimensioned name.

2 Using Implicit Variables

Visual Basic allows you to create variables automatically, without previously declaring or dimensioning them. A variable is an equation with an assigned name. When you create a variable without a previous definition, it is known as an implicit variable. Using implicit variables can lead to difficult-to-track errors due to the misspelling of a variable name. It is not good practice to use implicit variables—your application will be much easier to work with when you have complete control of all variables used in your application.

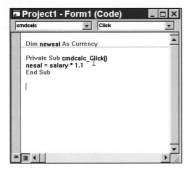

3 Using Explicit Variables

Visual Basic provides you with the ability of preventing such problems. When you add the **Option Explicit** statement to your Declaration Section, you are setting a condition that variables must be declared. Visual Basic will give you an error message when it encounters a variable which has not been declared.

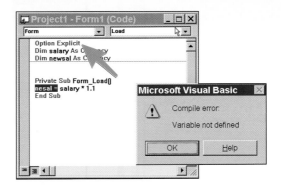

4 Using Variable Types

A variable can store almost any type of information. It can define numeric, string, or even True/False values called Booleans. As you can imagine, each type reserves a different amount of memory, and each has its own efficiencies associated with it.

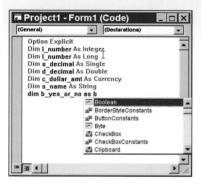

5 Using Constants

As you may have concluded, a variable can change from time to time during your application. When you need a variable that remains consistent, you create a constant. For example, if you were to set a security level based on the password login, that level would remain in effect throughout the entire application session. A constant requires less overhead and is more efficient then a variable.

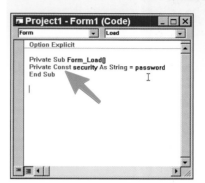

6 Using Variable Naming

Variables should be identifiable. Try to use descriptive names that will identify the type of variable and what information it stores. Variables should start with a letter and cannot contain spaces or special characters. Try to keep names unique, and avoid Visual Basic reserved names.

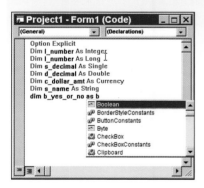

How-To Hints

Option Explicit

As previously mentioned, using the **Option Explicit** command is good practice and should be set as a default option. This will automatically add the **Option Explicit** statement in all your procedures.

End

TASK 2

How to Use Variables

You have just discovered what variables are and how to declare them. You now examine the different types of scopes associated with these variables, and how to use them in your application. The scope of a variable refers to where and when it is active and available in your application.

Begin

1 Using Local or Private Variables

A local variable, also known as a private variable, allows you to declare a variable at the procedure or module level. These variables are only available when you are in the procedure or module where it has been declared. A private variable is reset, or loses its value, when you leave the active procedure or module.

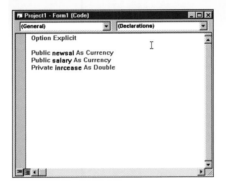

2 Using Public or Global Variables

A public variable, also known as a global variable, can be accessed throughout your application. Working with too many global variables increases the number of variables you have in each procedure. This can make it more difficult to debug and track variable values; therefore, you should try to use global variables only when it is necessary to have the variables available in all your procedures.

3 Using Static Variables

In some cases, you may have a local variable and you do not want it to be reset. You want to keep it active for the next time that it is called—this is called a static variable. An example would be a counter that you wanted to increment each time it was called.

84 CHAPTER 6: USING THE BASIC LANGUAGE

4 Using Variable Arrays

An array is when you have multiple occurrences of the same field. In some cases, it might be preferable to have more than one occurrence of a variable—for example, if you needed 12 variables for tracking monthly sales totals. Rather than creating a variable for each month, Visual Basic allows you to create an array of sales variables.

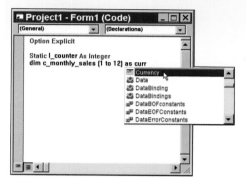

5 Pass Variable Data

Given the fact that working with local variables is more preferable than working with global ones, and local variables are only available by the procedure where they have been declared, you need a method of passing data. When a procedure has a variable and calls another process, it can pass arguments to the called routine.

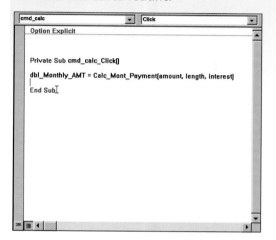

6 Receive a Variable

When you pass data to a called routine, the called routine must receive the data. Once the data has been passed, the called procedure now has control of the variable. If you apply a calculation or any changes to the variable, you must pass back the new value.

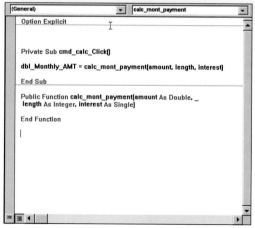

How-To Hints

Dimensioning Variables

It is always good practice to declare your variables. Besides avoiding the misspelling errors, the default type for a variable is called a variant and will accept any type of data. A variant reserves the greatest amount of memory and requires more overhead to determine the data type stored. Therefore, it's best to declare or reserve exactly what you need.

End

How to Select the Correct Variable

It is important that you select the correct variable type when you use variables. Utilizing the accurate variable type will speed up your application and reduce the amount of required overhead. In order to decide which variable to select, you need to know the limits of each variable option. This task shows the data that can be stored in a variable along with the boundaries for each.

Begin

1 Using Characters

String or alphanumeric characters can be stored in a variable type of string. You can enter any type of data into a string. The memory requirements are one character requires one byte of memory.

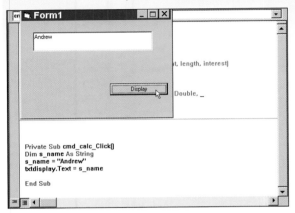

```
Private Sub cmd_calc_Click()
Dim s_name As String
s_name = "Andrew"
txtdisplay.Text = s_name

End Sub
```

2 Using Whole Numbers

There are two types of whole numbers that you can use. The first is called integers and requires less memory, uses two bytes, and has a small range. The valid range for an integer is –32,768 to 32,767. The second type of whole number is called long, and requires four bytes of memory and can store up to approximately (+/-) 2 billion.

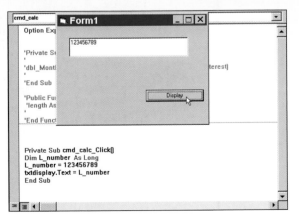

```
Private Sub cmd_calc_Click()
Dim L_number As Long
L_number = 123456789
txtdisplay.Text = L_number
End Sub
```

3 Using Decimal Numbers

As with whole numbers, there are two types of decimal numbers that you can use. The first is called single, and it uses four bytes of memory and will handle a range of (+/-) 1E-45 to 3E38. The double decimal type, requires eight bytes of memory and will deal with a range of (+/-) 5E-324 to 1.8E308. Both singles and doubles are floating-point decimal type variables.

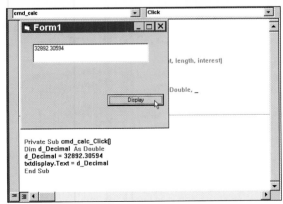

```
Private Sub cmd_calc_Click()
Dim d_Decimal As Double
d_Decimal = 32892.30594
txtdisplay.Text = d_Decimal
End Sub
```

4 Using Currency Variables

Currency variables need eight bytes of memory and manage a range of (+/-) 9E14. Currency data types use four fixed decimal places.

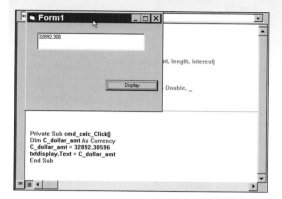

5 Using Date Variables

Date variables occupy eight bytes of memory. The date range is from January 1, 100 to December 31, 9999. The date variable contains the time of day as well as the full date.

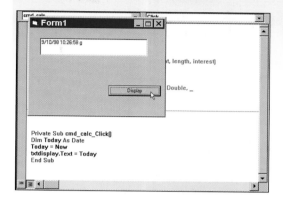

6 Using Boolean Variables

Boolean data types take two bytes of memory and they can only store one of two values. Boolean variables are used to specify a True or False state.

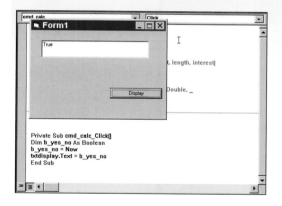

7 Choose the Output Format

Variable values are also used for displaying information. Visual Basic provides you with the capability of defining output or display options.

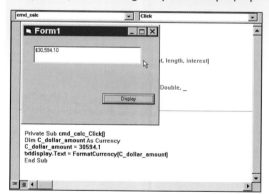

End

How-To Hints

Watch Out!

The use of an invalid amount in an integer field will cause an overflow error message.

How to Use Arithmetic Operators

The ability to perform mathematical operations in any programming language is vital to the processing of most applications. Visual Basic provides a number of mathematical operators that can be used in your code. In this task, you review the rules and symbols that Visual Basic uses to establish a valid mathematical equation.

Begin

1 Addition and Subtraction

The addition and subtraction of as many numbers as you want is accomplished by using the plus sign (+) for addition, and the minus sign (–) for subtraction. The functionality acts just as a calculator, where you can string multiple numbers together.

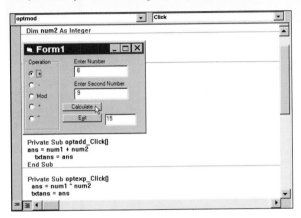

2 Multiplication

Multiplying as many numbers as you want works similar to the addition and subtraction operations. The multiplication symbol is an asterisk (*).

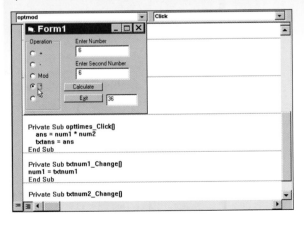

3 Division

Visual Basic provides you with several types of division. The first, regular division, is the same division that you were taught in school. Regular division provides full floating-point values to variables. The symbol used for division is a forward slash (/).

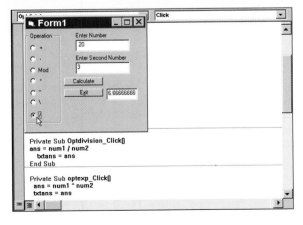

4 Integer Division

Integer division populates the variable with a whole number. When your formula results produce a remainder, the decimal portion will be dropped and your variable will contain the whole number only. The symbol for integer division is the backward slash (\).

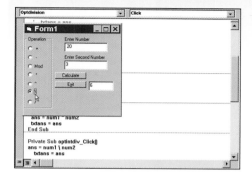

5 Mod Division

The converse of integer division is Mod division. This populates the variable with the rounded remainder of a division. The command for this operation is **Mod**.

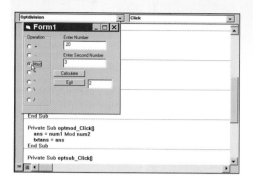

6 Exponents

Although the most frequently used functions are **Add**, **Subtract**, **Multiply**, and **Divide**, there is an additional function called an exponential calculation. The exponent symbol is the caret character (^). Visual Basic multiplies the number on the left of the caret by the power of the number to the right of the caret. As an example, 2^3 is the equivalent of 2*2*2.

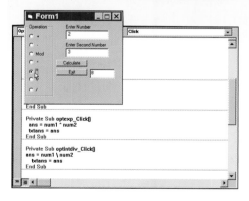

7 Operational Order

Visual Basic will not carry out your equation from left to right. As with all mathematical equations, the rules or order of execution determine which operations will be performed first. Visual Basic's hierarchy is exponents, multiplication, regular division, integer division, and mod division, followed by addition and subtraction.

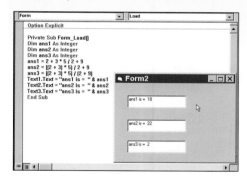

End

How to Use Basic Expressions

Now that you have reviewed variables and arithmetic symbols for calculations, you can generate a mathematical formula or expression. This task examines and reviews string manipulation and how to incorporate them in your expressions. You will also review a number of built-in functions, as well as date and time capability.

Begin

1 Assign a String

You can assign a value to a string variable by enclosing your string in double quotes (""). You can also assign the value of an inputbox or a textbox to your variable. Because these are not literal, you do not need the double quotes.

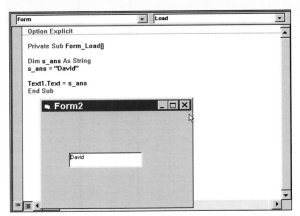

2 Concatenate a String

When you concatenate two strings, you are creating a new string that has both strings combined end to end. The concatenation symbol is the ampersand (&). You have the ability of concatenating alpha and numeric data in one string. This string will then be treated as an alpha variable, and can be used for displaying results of calculations.

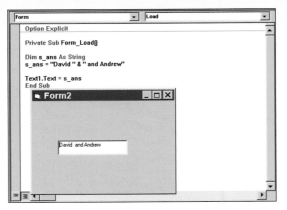

3 Manipulate a String

Visual Basic supplies you with multiple manipulation ability of strings. You can change the justification, extract portions, or change the format.

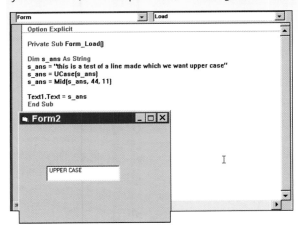

4 Choose a Date and Time Format

You have multiple options to choose from when working with date and time formats—from a long date format, which includes the day and date, to a short time format that only shows the minutes and seconds. The **Now** function will return today's date.

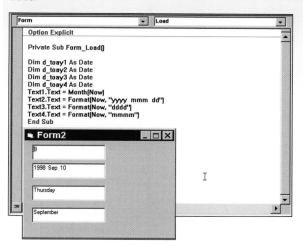

5 Manipulate Your Date

Date manipulation can be accomplished with additional built-in functions. **Dateadd** can be used to add or subtract a number of days and results in a new date. **Datediff** allows you to calculate the interval between two dates.

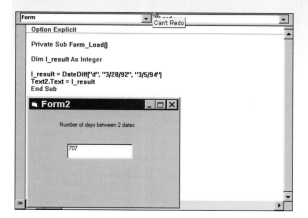

End

Task

7

Decision Making with Visual Basic

Visual Basic provides you with the ability to control the flow or direction of your application. The use of conditional statements will add to your ability to control your application. Conditional programming allows you to test for conditions and then execute a different section of code based on the results of the test. You will review Visual Basic's conditional programming techniques and how to use them. ●

How to Use If...Then...Else Statements

Using **If...Then...Else** logic not only allows you to control the flow of your application; you can control variables and data values as well. The **If** portion of the statement can be from a simple value comparison to a complex formula. Based on the **If** result, you can choose to change variable and data values, call functions, as well as display messages. You can even combine **If...Then...Else** in response to a message box. This section will cover how the **If...Then...Else** logic works.

Begin

1 Using If...Then

If...Then logic allows you to execute a section of code or set conditions when the **If** condition is true. The format itself really explains the concept. If a condition is true, then perform code. If the condition is false, Visual Basic will ignore the **Then** step.

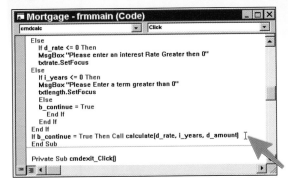

2 Using If...Then...Else

If...Then...Else logic is similar in concept to **If...Then**; however, **If...Then...Else** allows you to create a more complex testing condition. If you do not encounter a true condition, the **Else** code will be executed.

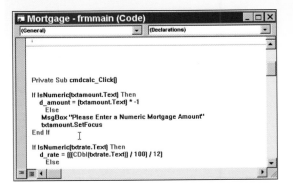

3 Using ElseIf (Multiple If Conditions)

ElseIf allows you to continue the **If...Then...Else** testing. You can also test for several different true conditions, and perform different code for each one.

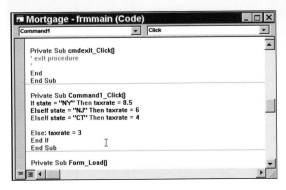

4 Using EndIf

An **EndIf** command is required at the end of an **If...Then** if it spans multiple lines or an **If...Then...Else** condition. This allows Visual Basic to determine when the conditions have ended.

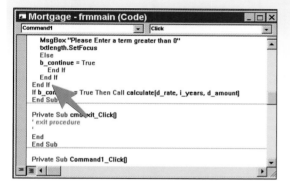

```
Mortgage - frmmain (Code)
Command1                        Click
        MsgBox "Please Enter a term greater than 0"
        txtlength.SetFocus
        Else
        b_continue = True
            End If
        End If
    End If
    If b_con     = True Then Call calculate(d_rate, i_years, d_amount)
    End Sub

    Private Sub cmd_xit_Click()
    ' exit procedure

    End
    End Sub

    Private Sub Command1_Click()
```

5 Know When to Stop

When you are using multiple **If** conditions, Visual Basic will process the **If** conditions one at a time until it reaches a true condition and then go to the **EndIf**. With that in mind, you need to structure your conditions in the correct order.

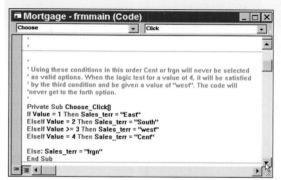

```
Mortgage - frmmain (Code)
Choose                          Click

' Using these conditions in this order Cent or frgn will never be selected
' as valid options. When the logic test for a value of 4, it will be satisfied
' by the third condition and be given a value of "west". The code will
'never get to the forth option.

Private Sub Choose_Click()
If Value = 1 Then Sales_terr = "East"
ElseIf Value = 2 Then Sales_terr = "South"
ElseIf Value >= 3 Then Sales_terr = "west"
ElseIf Value = 4 Then Sales_terr = "Cent"

Else: Sales_terr = "frgn"
End Sub
```

End

How-To Hints

More Than One

If you use more than one **If...Then** on the same line, an **EndIf** statement is not required.

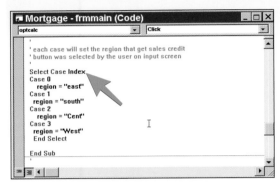

How to Use Select Case

An alternative to the **If...Then...Else** logic is **Select Case** logic. Using **Select Case** makes your code easier to read and understand. When you have a condition that can be satisfied by multiple cases, the first satisfied case will be executed. When you use the **Select Case** code, the condition is supplied once; with **If...Then...Else**, the condition is supplied with each **If**.

Begin

1 Using the Select Case Statement

The **Select Case** statement includes an argument to be tested. The tested argument value represents the case that will be executed. The argument can be a valid number or string expression.

2 Choose Case Name

The **Case** name represents the possible values for the argument. The **Case** name will be compared to the argument. This is one of the differences from **If...Then...Else**, which can be compared to different values, and not at the same time.

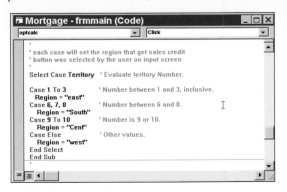

3 Using Case Code

When a **Case** name satisfies the argument value, the code for that **Case** will be executed. When a satisfactory condition is met, the remaining **Case** name will not be tested.

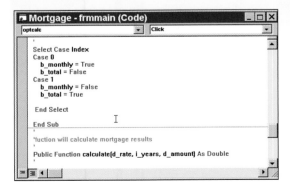

4 Using Case Else

Case logic has a **Case Else** clause. The code contained under this **Case** will be executed if no other **Case** successfully satisfies the condition. This **Case** is added as the last case.

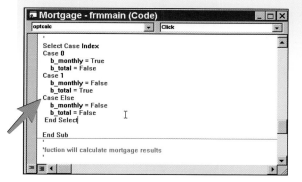

5 Using End Select

This command is added to the end of the **Case** logic and tells Visual Basic that there are no more cases to process. This is where processing is continued after a **Case** has been successfully met and its code processed.

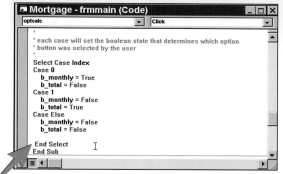

End

How-To Hints

More Logic

If you need to examine two different arguments or change arguments, you must use **If...Then...Else** logic.

How to Use Looping

When you need to execute a block of code repetitively, Visual Basic has several looping capabilities. You can use counter or conditional looping. With a counter loop, you can instruct Visual Basic how many times to repeat the code. In conditional loops, you control the loop until a condition occurs. The basic concept of a loop is to repeat a block of code until a condition interrupts the looping. These loops and the looping strategies available will be reviewed in this task.

Begin

1 Using Do While...Loop

Do While...Loop conditional looping executes while a condition is true. When the condition is no longer true, the looping will end. When the **Loop** statement is encountered, it will return to the **Do** statement again.

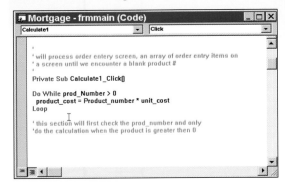

2 Using Do...Loop While

The **Do...Loop While** loop is very similar to **Do While...Loop**. It also executes while a condition exists or is true; the major difference between the two is that the **While** statement appears after the code. This will actually process the code at least once before the **While** is tested.

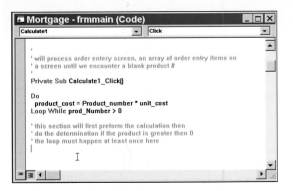

3 Using Do Until...Loop

Again, the concept is the same as **While**; the difference is that **Do Until...Loop** continues until a condition becomes true. So while a condition is false, the looping will continue. When the **Loop** statement is encountered, it returns to the **Do** statement again.

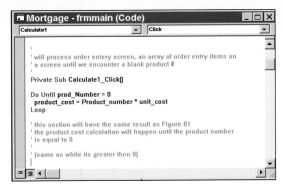

4 Using Do...Loop Until

By now you can probably guess that **Do...Loop Until** functions the same as **Do Until...Loop**. The code will continue to loop while the condition is false or until a condition becomes true. Once again, the difference is that this will execute the code at least once prior to testing the condition.

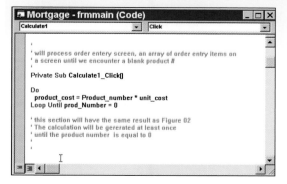

```
Mortgage - frmmain (Code)
Calculate1                          Click

    '
    ' will process order entery screen, an array of order entry items on
    ' a screen until we encounter a blank product #
    '
    Private Sub Calculate1_Click()

    Do
      product_cost = Product_number * unit_cost
    Loop Until prod_Number = 0

    ' this section will have the same result as Figure 02
    ' The calculation will be gererated at least once
    ' until the product number  is equal to 0
    '
    '
```

5 Using Loops

As previously mentioned, the **Loop** statement represents the end of the looping cycle. This statement will send the process back to the beginning of the loop, or evaluate whether the condition will end the looping process.

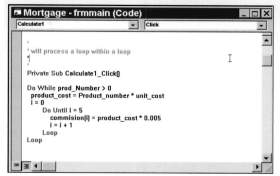

```
Mortgage - frmmain (Code)
Calculate1                          Click

    '
    ' will process a loop within a loop
    '
    Private Sub Calculate1_Click()

    Do While prod_Number > 0
      product_cost = Product_number * unit_cost
      i = 0
        Do Until i = 5
          commision(i) = product_cost * 0.005
          i = i + 1
        Loop
    Loop
```

End

How-To Hints

Conditional Looping

Conditional looping is used when you are not sure how many times you need to repeat code.

TASK 4

How to Use Looping, Part II

You have just reviewed looping based on conditions for true or false values. This looping is based on variable or data conditions. You really don't have control over how many times the code will repeat. Now you examine loops that are based on a number, where you control the repetition of the code.

Begin

1 Using For...Next

You use **For...Next** when you know how many times you want to repeat a block of code. With **For...Next**, you are in complete control of how often code will be repeated. The **For...Next** concept is applying code against transaction or array data. As the next element in the array, or record in the database, is read, the code will be executed.

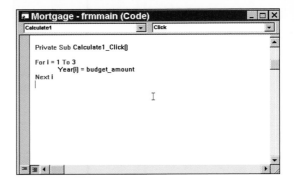

2 Using Next

The **For** statement instructs Visual Basic how many times a section of code should be repeated. The section ends with the **Next** statement. The **Next** statement, which is followed by a counter variable, is incremented and the code repeated. This will continue until the code has been executed the required number of times.

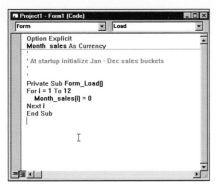

3 Using For Each...Next

For Each...Next acts identical to the **For...Next** loop; however, it does not work off a counter. This works on a collection of items. You might not even know how many items exist. For example, you can read all your database records into an array. For each item in the array, the section of code will be executed.

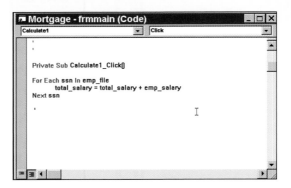

4 Using Next Element

The **For...Each** statement ends with the **Next** element statement. The **Next** element statement will select the next element in your array, and the code is repeated. This will continue until all the data in your array has been reviewed.

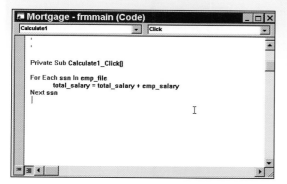

```
Mortgage - frmmain (Code)
Calculate1                    Click

'
'
Private Sub Calculate1_Click()

For Each ssn In emp_file
        total_salary = total_salary + emp_salary
Next ssn
```

5 Using Exit For

When you use the **For Each** logic, you are stepping through your data. In some cases, you may need to exit your loop prior to reading through your entire data. You can leave your loop with the **Exit For** statement.

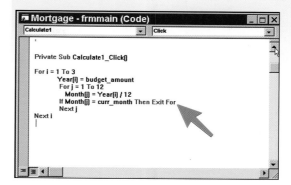

```
Mortgage - frmmain (Code)
Calculate1                    Click

'
Private Sub Calculate1_Click()

For i = 1 To 3
        Year(i) = budget_amount
        For j = 1 To 12
            Month(j) = Year(i) / 12
            If Month(j) = curr_month Then Exit For
        Next j
Next i
```

6 Using Nesting For

Visual Basic allows you to nest the **For Each** statement block. Nesting is when you have a **For Each** within another **For Each**. For example, if you wanted to initialize two years of monthly sales amounts, you could have a **For Each** for the 12 months within a **For Each** for the three years.

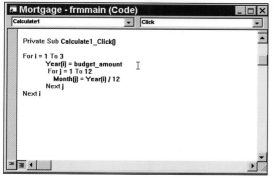

```
Mortgage - frmmain (Code)
Calculate1                    Click

'
Private Sub Calculate1_Click()

For i = 1 To 3
        Year(i) = budget_amount
        For j = 1 To 12
            Month(j) = Year(i) / 12
        Next j
Next i
```

End

How-To Hints

Variant

When you use the **For Each** loop to access an array, the data type must be **Variant**.

Looping Decrement

When you use looping with stepping criteria, the loop will continue until the value of the endpoint is reached. This can also be reversed: Loop until you reach zero and subtract from a starting point.

Project

In the project, you review the arithmetic functions and the `If...Then...Else` logic. In this project, you will create a mortgage calculator. The project contains the options of calculating the monthly payment or calculating the total amount paid for the life of the loan. You will allow for three inputs, including the loan amount, interest rate, and length of time of the loan.

1 Start a New Project

Choose **Project**, **New Project** from the VB menu. Select the **Standard EXE** option from the **New** tab of the Visual Basic **New Project** screen. **Name** the form **frmmain** and give it the **Caption** of **Mortgage Calculator**. Increase the size of the screen.

2 Add a Command Button

Select the **Command Button** control icon from the **Toolbox**, and add it to the form. **Name** the button **cmdcalc** and give it the **Caption** of **&Calculate**.

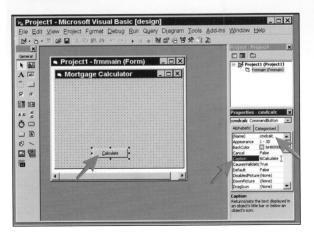

3 Add an Exit Button

Now add a second command button to the right of the first command button. **Name** the button **cmdexit** and give it a **Caption** of **E&xit**.

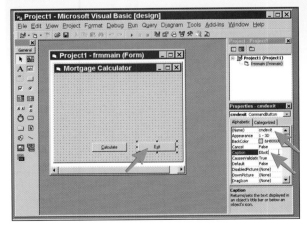

4 Provide an Amount Textbox

Double-click the **TextBox** control icon in the **Toolbox** to add a textbox to the form. **Name** it **txtamount** and blank out the text description.

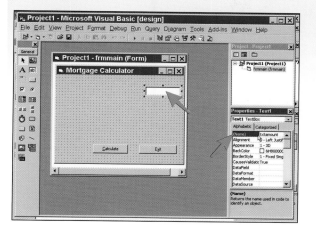

5 Add a Rate Textbox

Add another textbox to the form and position it under the first textbox. **Name** this textbox **txtrate**, and again blank out the text description.

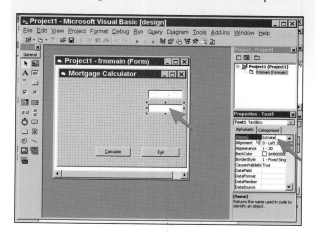

6 Add a Length-of-Time Textbox

Now add a final textbox from the **Toolbox**, and position it under the previous textbox. **Name** the textbox **txtlength**, and blank out the text description.

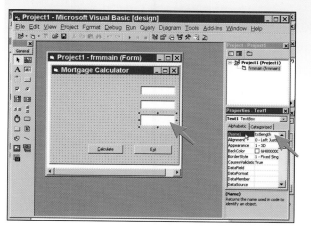

7 Create Labels for the Textboxes

Select the **Label** icon from the **Toolbox** and add a label to the right of each textbox. **Caption** each with the captions **Mortgage Amount**, **Interest Rate**, and **Number of Years**.

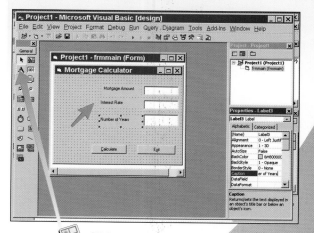

Click

Continues

8 Create a Frame

From the **Toolbox**, select the **Frame** control button and give it a **Caption** of **Calculation Type**.

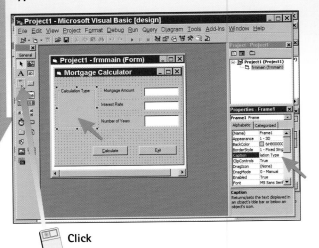

Click

9 Make a Monthly Option Button

Add an option button to the frame by clicking the **Option Button** control icon in the the **Toolbox**. Give it a **Name** of **optcalc**, and a **Caption** of **Monthly Payment**.

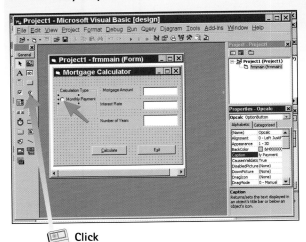

Click

10 Add a Total Button

Now add a second option button to your frame, giving it the same **Name** of **optcalc**. You can see that Visual Basic asks you if you want this to be an array. Select **Yes**. **Caption** the second button as **Total Amount Paid**.

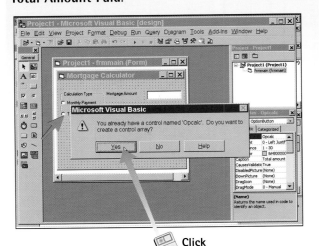

Click

11 Save Your Work

Remember to periodically save your work. Select **Project Properties** under the **Project** menu to call up the **Project Properties** dialog. Under the **General** tab, change the **Startup Object** to **frmmain**.

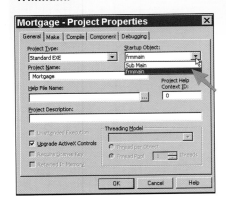

12 Provide a Project Title

Next, move to the **Make** tab and change the **Title** to **Mortgage Calculator**. Now click **OK**.

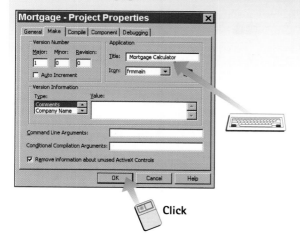

Click

13 Add Code

It's time to add and review the code. Click the **View Code** icon in the **Project window**.

Click

14 Add the Option Explicit Command

If it does not already exist, add the **Option Explicit** command. Dimension the following variables under **Option Explicit**; this will reserve space for these values in memory.

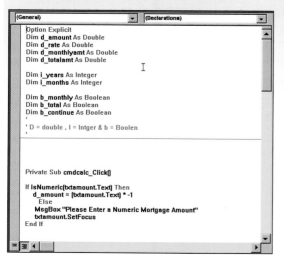

```
(General)                    (Declarations)

Option Explicit
Dim d_amount As Double
Dim d_rate As Double
Dim d_monthlyamt As Double
Dim d_totalamt As Double

Dim i_years As Integer
Dim i_months As Integer

Dim b_monthly As Boolean
Dim b_total As Boolean
Dim b_continue As Boolean
'
' D = double , I = Intger & b = Boolen
'


Private Sub cmdcalc_Click()

If IsNumeric(txtamount.Text) Then
    d_amount = (txtamount.Text) * -1
    Else
    MsgBox "Please Enter a Numeric Mortgage Amount"
    txtamount.SetFocus
End If
```

15 Enter the End Command

Select the **cmdexit_Click()** from the object and procedure drop-downs, and enter the **End** command.

```
cmdexit                      Click

Private Sub cmdexit_Click()
' exit procedure
'
End
End Sub

Private Sub Form_Load()
txtamount.Text = "000.00"
txtrate.Text = "0.000"
txtlength.Text = "00"
optcalc(0).Value = True
b_monthly = True
b_continue = False
End Sub

Private Sub optcalc_Click(Index As Integer)

Select Case Index
Case 0
    b_monthly = True
    b_total = False
Case 1
    b_monthly = False
    b_total = True
End Select

End Sub
```

Continues

Project Continued

16 Set Defaults

Select the **Form_Load** options and set these default values.

```
Form                    ▼  Load                    ▼
    Private Sub Form_Load()
    'set default amounts
    txtamount.Text = "000.00"          I
    txtrate.Text = "0.000"
    txtlength.Text = "00"
    ' this sets the default option button
    optcalc(0).Value = True
    'this Boolean variables  sets default to calculate the monthly payment
    b_monthly = True
    'This Boolean variable is set to false, data validation has not taken place
    'it will be set to true after the data has been validated
    b_continue = False
    End Sub

    Private Sub optcalc_Click(Index As Integer)

    Select Case Index
    Case 0
       b_monthly = True
       b_total = False
    Case 1
       b_monthly = False
       b_total = True
    End Select

    End Sub

    Public Function calculate(d_rate, i_years, d_amount) As Double
```

17 Calculate the Code

Now, select **cmdcalc_Click()** and enter the following code. This code will check each entry and validate that the user supplied numeric data. The application is also preparing the numbers for the calculations by converting the alpha strings to numeric.

The **SetFocus** command instructs the cursor where to return to if an error occurs.

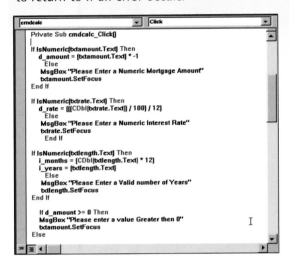

```
cmdcalc                 ▼  Click                   ▼
    Private Sub cmdcalc_Click()
    |
    If IsNumeric(txtamount.Text) Then
        d_amount = (txtamount.Text) * -1
       Else
        MsgBox "Please Enter a Numeric Mortgage Amount"
        txtamount.SetFocus
    End If

    If IsNumeric(txtrate.Text) Then
        d_rate = (((CDbl(txtrate.Text)) / 100) / 12)
        Else
        MsgBox "Please Enter a Numeric Interest Rate"
        txtrate.SetFocus
        End If

    If IsNumeric(txtlength.Text) Then
        i_months = (CDbl(txtlength.Text) * 12)
        i_years = (txtlength.Text)
        Else
        MsgBox "Please Enter a Valid number of Years"
        txtlength.SetFocus
    End If

       If d_amount >= 0 Then
        MsgBox "Please enter a value Greater then 0"     I
        txtamount.SetFocus
       Else
```

18 Set Boolean Values

The next lines of code, also in **cmdcalc_Click()**, test that the values are greater than zero. The Boolean variable **b_continue** is set to false until all the validation is complete. When **b_continue** is true, it will call a procedure and pass variables.

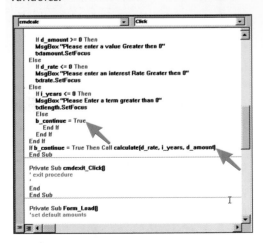

```
cmdcalc                 ▼  Click                   ▼
       If d_amount >= 0 Then
        MsgBox "Please enter a value Greater then 0"
        txtamount.SetFocus
       Else
        If d_rate <= 0 Then
        MsgBox "Please enter an interest Rate Greater then 0"
        txtrate.SetFocus
       Else
        If i_years <= 0 Then
        MsgBox "Please Enter a term greater than 0"
        txtlength.SetFocus
        Else
        b_continue = True
          End If
        End If
       End If
    If b_continue = True Then Call calculate(d_rate, i_years, d_amount)
    End Sub

    Private Sub cmdexit_Click()
    ' exit procedure
    '
    End
    End Sub

    Private Sub Form_Load()                          I
    'set default amounts
```

19 Add a Function

From the **Tools** menu, select **Add Procedure**, and add a public function named **calculate** from the **Add Procedure** dialog box. Remember to save your project from time to time.

```
Add Procedure                          ☒
  Name:  calculate          ┌──────────┐
                            │    OK    │
  ┌─Type──────────────┐    └──────────┘
  │ ○ Sub   ○ Property │    ┌──────────┐
  │ ● Function ○ Event │    │  Cancel  │
  └───────────────────┘    └──────────┘
  ┌─Scope─────────────┐
  │ ● Public ○ Private │
  └───────────────────┘
  ☐ All Local variables as Statics
```

20 Test User Input

Accept the variables that are passed to the function, and add this code. This will determine whether the user wants to calculate the monthly payment schedule or the total amount paid. It uses Boolean variables. **Pmt** is a predefined function in Visual Basic that calculates mortgages.

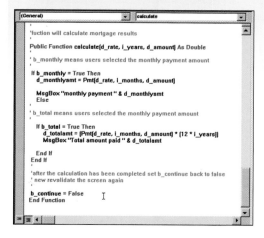

```
(General)                        ▼   calculate                    ▼
'
'fuction will calculate mortgage results
'
Public Function calculate(d_rate, i_years, d_amount) As Double
'
' b_monthly means users selected the monthly payment amount
'
If b_monthly = True Then
    d_monthlyamt = Pmt(d_rate, i_months, d_amount)

    MsgBox "monthly payment " & d_monthlyamt
Else
'
' b_total means users selected the monthly payment amount
'
    If b_total = True Then
        d_totalamt = (Pmt(d_rate, i_months, d_amount) * (12 * i_years))
        MsgBox "Total amount paid " & d_totalamt

    End If
End If
'
'after the calculation has been completed set b_continue back to false
' new revalidate the screen again
'
b_continue = False
End Function
```

21 Object Arrays

Next select **optcalc_Click()**; notice that because this is an array, Visual Basic has added **Index As Integer** in the parentheses. This was done because the index value will uniquely identify which of the same name options has been selected. Here, you add the **Select Case** logic.

You are using Boolean variables to determine which case has been selected. You could have used only one variable and tested for a false condition. However, for this example you are using separate variables to show that they must be reset.

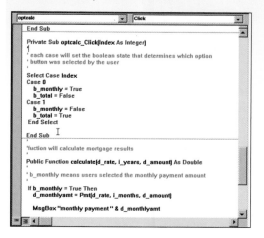

```
optcalc                          ▼   Click                        ▼
End Sub

Private Sub optcalc_Click(Index As Integer)
'
' each case will set the boolean state that determines which option
' button was selected by the user
'
Select Case Index
Case 0
    b_monthly = True
    b_total = False
Case 1
    b_monthly = False
    b_total = True
End Select

End Sub

'fuction will calculate mortgage results
'
Public Function calculate(d_rate, i_years, d_amount) As Double
'
' b_monthly means users selected the monthly payment amount
'
If b_monthly = True Then
    d_monthlyamt = Pmt(d_rate, i_months, d_amount)

    MsgBox "monthly payment " & d_monthlyamt
```

22 Test the Application

Run your application and test the results.

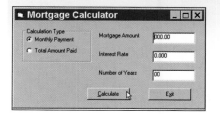

23 Make and Run an Executable

Create an .EXE which can run on its own. Click the **File** menu and select **Make Project.EXE** to create an executable file. Find the EXE file and double-click it.

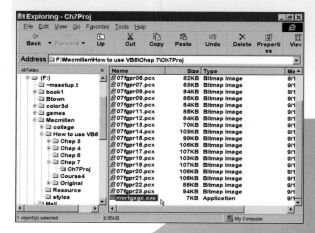

End

Task

Subroutines and Functions

*C*reating applications requires that you write many lines of program code that instruct the computer on how to process the information that will be entered. In many cases, you will be repeating large amounts of code in different areas of the program, which makes it very hard to make changes when they are needed. Procedures give you the ability to centralize this code and execute it from wherever it is needed, reducing the amount of code you need to maintain.

Two of the most common elements of a Visual Basic program are the subroutine and function. These procedures are used to perform a certain task and return control to the program that called it. A function is a specialized form of a subroutine that can return a value to the calling program. Both subroutines and functions can be passed variables, and both accept the same types of arguments. Using these procedures make it easier for you to code, test, and debug your program because it reduces the amount of code that you have to look at. ●

How to Add a Procedure to the Project

A subroutine and a function are both considered procedures in Visual Basic. While you can add a procedure to a form, most procedures are added to a separate file called a Code Module. This task will show you how to add both subroutines and functions to your project.

Begin

1 Add a Code Module

Right-click in the **Project Explorer**, and then select **Add** and choose **Module** from the pop-up menu.

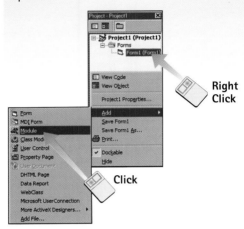

2 Select the Code Module

Select **Module** from the **New** tab in the **Add Module** dialog box, and click **Open**.

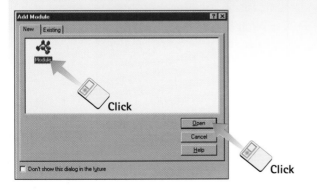

3 Add a Procedure

Drop down the **Tools** menu and choose **Add Procedure**.

4 Name the Procedure

Enter the procedure name in the **Name** textbox of the **Add Procedure** dialog box.

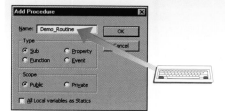

5 Specify the Procedure Type

The **Procedure Type** radio buttons specifies whether it is a subroutine or a function. Depending on the type of procedure you want, you would select one of these two options.

 Click

End

How-To Hints

Subroutines vs. Functions

If a subroutine or a function is declared as **Public**, it can be executed from anywhere in the application. However, if it is declared as **Private**, it can only be accessed from the module it was declared in. Only functions will return a value to the calling routine, while subroutines require global variables to store the modified data.

How to Pass Arguments

Arguments are the variables that procedures can use within their code. They are passed to the procedure during the execution of the **Call** statement of reference to the function. There are actually three different ways for a procedure to use variables and data in an application.

Begin

1 Using Public Variables

There are several different types of variables you can declare in your application. The most common of these are **Public** variables. These can be accessed from any form or procedure in the application. This allows you to set a variable in the main code and then modify it in a procedure.

2 Passing Variables by Reference

Passing variables to a procedure by reference is a lot like using **Public** variables. When you change them in a procedure, they are changed in the main code as well. The only real difference is that you can change the name of the variable in the procedure.

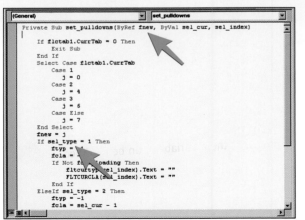

3 Passing Variables by Value

Another method for passing a variable is by value to the procedure; and if none is specified, the by value method is assumed to be the default. This allows you to work with the values without changing the original data.

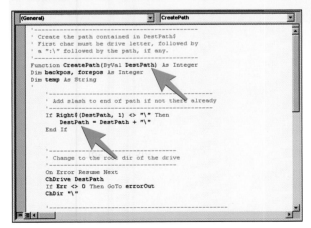

4 Returning Data in a Function

Functions generally pass variable data by value and then return the answer in the function name.

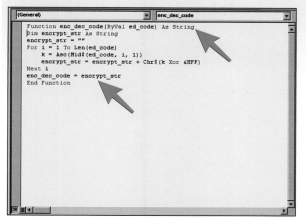

```
(General)                              ▼    enc_dec_code                    ▼

    Function enc_dec_code(ByVal ed_code) As String
    Dim encrypt_str As String
    encrypt_str = ""
    For i = 1 To Len(ed_code)
        k = Asc(Mid$(ed_code, i, 1))
        encrypt_str = encrypt_str + Chr$(k Xor &HFF)
    Next i
    enc_dec_code = encrypt_str
    End Function
```

End

How-To Hints

ByRef vs. ByVal

Using variables passed by value is much safer for your program code than using variables passed by reference, because this prevents your program code from accidentally modifying a value that should not be changed.

Returning Data in a Subroutine

If you are using a subroutine and require that data be passed between the routine and the main program code, you should define **Public** variables and access them from both the main code and the subroutine. However, you must remember that these variables can be modified anywhere in the program.

How to Use a Subroutine or Function

Subroutines allow you to have one section of code that can be used from anywhere in the application. Placing code within a subroutine makes the application easier to test and makes it easier for you to find problems. The process of using a procedure is basically creating the procedure and then writing the code to perform the required action.

Begin

1 Add Code to a Subroutine

The code for a subroutine is nothing more than a given section of code moved from the main program code area to within the subroutine **Sub...End Sub** statements.

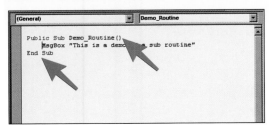

2 Code a Function

Functions are a little different from subroutines because functions return values. This is done by assigning the value to the name of the function.

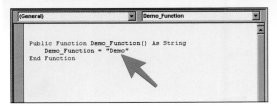

3 Execute a Subroutine

Subroutines are executed using the **Call** statement from within the main program code. When this statement is encountered, execution is transferred from the main code to the beginning of the subroutine code. Then when the subroutine is finished, execution returns to the next statement following the **Call**.

4 Use a Function

A function must be executed as part of another statement, such as an assignment statement. It can also be used as a variable to another function or procedure.

5 Using a Function as a Parameter

Because a function can return a value from within the routine, functions are frequently used as parameters for other functions.

End

How-To Hints

Using Procedures

Using procedures in your application is a double-edged sword. By including procedures, you will reduce the amount of code that you have to maintain. However, because of the way execution is transferred to the procedure and then back to the main code, it will eventually impact the performance of a complex application.

Task

9

Working with Arrays and Collections

Most computer programs manipulate many different variables during their processing. Arrays give you the ability to work with a group of variables of the same type that are referred to by a common name. By using an array, you would not need to work with many unique named variables. To keep track of 100 names, you would either need 100 separate variables or one 100 element array.

Arrays come in many different shapes and sizes. In fact, Visual Basic and Windows make use of a special type of array called a control collection. This collection allows you to work with objects such as controls and forms. An example of a collection could be a data entry form with 10 textboxes on it that are accessed using a single control array. In addition, you can also define your own collections that contain any data type that you need to store.

In this chapter, you are going to see how to define an array, how to store and retrieve data in it, and finally how to use processing loops to perform this task. You will also learn how to create a control array, how to create a custom collection in Visual Basic, and how to access it. ●

How to Define a Single Dimension Array

A simple array is declared in much the same way as a standard variable. The only real difference is specifying the number of unique values or elements that are in the array. This task shows you several different ways of defining the array and how to place data into it.

Begin

1 Start a New Project

Start a new project by choosing **New Project** from the **File** menu, and then choosing **Standard EXE** from the **New Project** dialog box. Click **OK**.

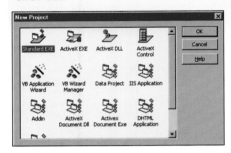

2 Add a Code Module

Right-click in the **Project Explorer** window, select **Add**, and choose **Module** from the pop-up menu. Then select **New Module** from the dialog box.

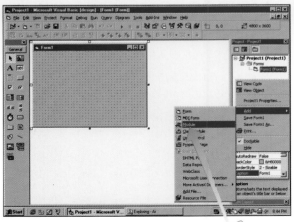

Click

3 Display the Declarations Section

An array is usually defined in the declarations of a form or module. To display the Declarations section, select the module in the **Project Explorer** and click the **View Code** button.

Click

4 Define a Simple Array

An array is defined using the **Dim** statement and by including the element count in parentheses. In addition, you can define an array using **Public** or **Private** depending on the requirements of your program.

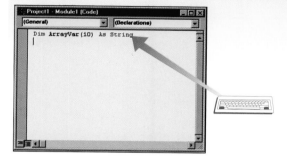

5 Designate the Starting Number

An array can start at any number. By default, all arrays start at zero. However, this can sometimes be confusing. By using the **Option Base** statement, you can specify the default start to one or zero.

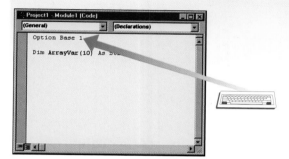

6 Specify a Starting Number

Besides setting the default starting value, you can also set the starting number when defining the array.

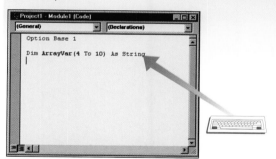

7 Using a Loop to Access the Array

To access an array, you can use a **For Loop** to access each element in the array as shown in the **Form Load** event routine.

End

How-To Hints

Setting a Data Type

Although you do not have to specify a data type for an array, you should remember that an array can contain only one data type. The way around this is to define a user data type that can contain any number of data types within it.

How to Define a Multidimensional Array

A simple or single-dimensional array is useful to contain a single column of data. The second type of array is a multidimensional array. This allows you to add two, three, or more dimensions to an array. An example of a multidimensional array is a chessboard that has eight rows and eight columns. To track the name and number of 100 people, you would need two separate simple arrays or one two-dimensional array.

Begin

1 Define a Two-Dimensional Array

To define an array that will hold names and numbers, you would use the code shown in the following figure.

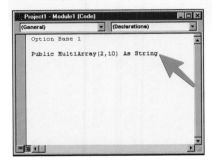

2 Set the Starting Point

As with simple arrays, you can specify the starting position when defining it.

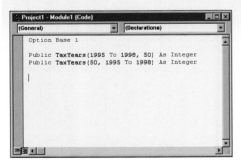

3 Store Data in an Array

To access any element in the array, you would specify the element number or subscript when using the array. The following example will store a string in the first element of the array.

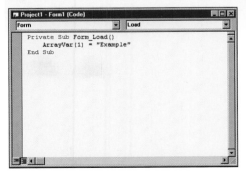

4 Using the Array Function

As you can probably guess from the previous step, if you need to initialize a large array, it will mean a large amount of typing. The **Array** function is an easy method you can use to create and load an array in one step.

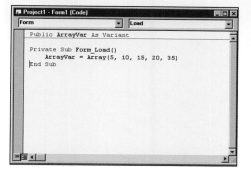

```
Public ArrayVar As Variant

Private Sub Form_Load()
    ArrayVar = Array(5, 10, 15, 20, 35)
End Sub
```

5 Using LBound and UBound

Because you can specify what the starting value of an array or lower bound is, you can use the **LBound** function to get the starting number of any dimension in an array using the following syntax:

```
X = Lbound(ArrayName, Dimension)
```

This allows you to write code that reacts to the number of elements in the array. The **UBound** function works the same way as the **LBound** function does, except **UBound** returns the ending value of an array, or the upper bound.

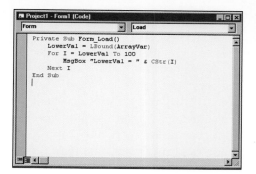

```
Private Sub Form_Load()
    LowerVal = LBound(ArrayVar)
    For I = LowerVal To 100
        MsgBox "LowerVal = " & CStr(I)
    Next I
End Sub
```

6 Access a Multidimensional Array

Arrays can be used to access data from a multidimensional array by nesting the same number of for loops as dimensions. The following code shown in the **Code Editor** is an example of how you can access the array.

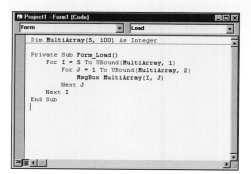

```
Dim MultiArray(5, 100) As Integer

Private Sub Form_Load()
    For I = 5 To UBound(MultiArray, 1)
        For J = 1 To UBound(MultiArray, 2)
            MsgBox MultiArray(I, J)
        Next J
    Next I
End Sub
```

End

How-To Hints

Redimensioning an Array

When using arrays, you can even change the number of elements dynamically during the execution of the program using the **ReDim** statement. This statement allows you to change the number of elements of the array. If you want to save the values already in the array, you would need to use the **Preserve** keyword in addition to the **ReDim** statement. The following syntax shows how to **ReDim** an array and preserve the data:

```
ReDim Preserve ArrayVar(50,500)
```

How to Work with a Collection

Collections play an important role in the programming of Visual Basic applications. They are always present and are maintained automatically as things change in the application. The advantages of using a collection rather than an array is that a collection will add new elements to it without having to code anything special as you do with a standard array. Finally, a collection can contain any data type, which allows you to have a collection that holds many different data types at the same time.

Begin

1 Define the Collection Name

When using a collection in your program, you must manage it yourself. The first step is to define the collection by using the **Collection** object in a **Public** statement.

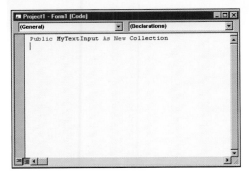

2 Add an Object

The **Add** method is used to add a new element or object to a collection. In addition to the data value, you can also specify a key along with the value—for example, adding a name and the associated Social Security number. This key can be used to access the name directly.

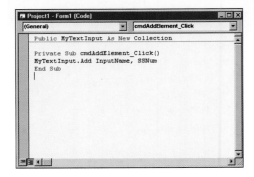

3 Remove an Object

You can to delete an element from the **Collection** by using the **Remove** method as shown.

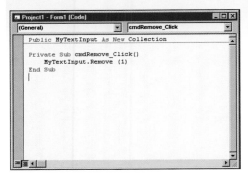

4 Specify the Item

The **Item** property is used to specify the element that you want to use.

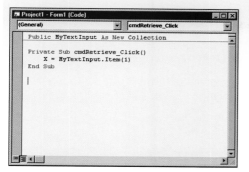

```
Public MyTextInput As New Collection

Private Sub cmdRetrieve_Click()
    X = MyTextInput.Item(1)
End Sub
```

5 Using the Count Property

The **Count** property is used to determine the current number of elements in the collection. This allows you to code a **For Loop** that works no matter how many elements there are.

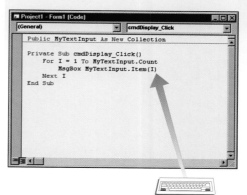

```
Public MyTextInput As New Collection

Private Sub cmdDisplay_Click()
    For I = 1 To MyTextInput.Count
        MsgBox MyTextInput.Item(I)
    Next I
End Sub
```

End

How-To Hints

Collection Usage

Even though creating and using a collection is easier than using a standard array, it has one disadvantage that an array doesn't. Because a collection can contain any data type, you must check to see which data type a collection element has before using it, unless all of the elements in the collection are the same. You control this within your application:

```
If TypeOf MyControl Is CommandButton Then
    Msgbox "This is a Command Button Control"
End If
```

TASK 4

How to Use a Control Array

Besides creating your own collection object that you can use as an array, you can also make use of the automatic control array that is handled by Visual Basic. Whenever you copy a control and then paste it on the same form, a control array is automatically created.

Begin

1 Add a Textbox to the Form

Add a textbox to the form by double-clicking the **TextBox** control button in the **Toolbox**.

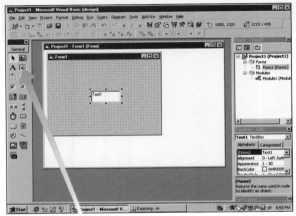

Double
Click

2 Copy the Textbox

Right-click the textbox and choose the **Copy** option from the pop-up menu.

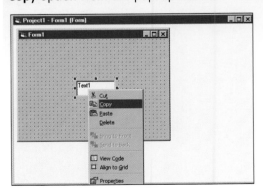

3 Paste the Textbox

When you paste the textbox on the form, you will see a message box informing you that you are about to create a control array.

4 Access the Array in an Event

Whenever you use control arrays, Visual Basic automatically adds an index parameter to each of the control's events.

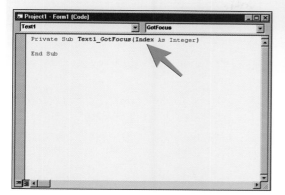

```
Private Sub Text1_GotFocus(Index As Integer)

End Sub
```

5 Access the Array

Once a control array is created, each object can be accessed by specifying its element number or index value.

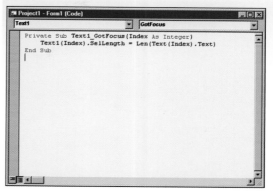

```
Private Sub Text1_GotFocus(Index As Integer)
    Text1(Index).SelLength = Len(Text(Index).Text)
End Sub
```

End

How-To Hints

Multiple Controls

A control array allows you to group liked controls together and create the code for those controls only once, using the **Index** property to specify which control is being accessed. This reduces the size of the program file and the amount of maintenance you would need to perform on the code if it was duplicated for each control.

Task

CHAPTER 10

Interfacing with the Mouse and Keyboard

*T*he Windows environment was created to make it easier for someone to interact with a computer application. The two main ways a user can interact with an application are by using the mouse and keyboard. In most situations, the standard processing for these input devices is enough for you to work with. An example of this is a textbox that accepts input from the keyboard or a command button that recognizes when the mouse clicked it.

However, in most applications that you create, you will probably need a way of intercepting the input from the mouse or keyboard before the automatic process is completed to perform some unique action, such as displaying a message to the user. Both the mouse and keyboard have several events associated with them that tell you what action the user has taken. This chapter shows you the different events and how you would use them in a Visual Basic program. ●

How to Use the MouseMove Event

In many applications, the position or location of the mouse is used to either perform a given task or to inform the user of a particular action. This is done using the **MouseMove** event. Almost every object or control in Visual Basic has this event associated with it. To see how this works, you will add a Label and TextBox control to a new project and have the program display a message in the label when the mouse moves over the textbox.

Begin

1 Start a New Project

Pull down the **File** menu and choose **New**. Then, select **Standard EXE** on the **New Project** dialog and click **OK**.

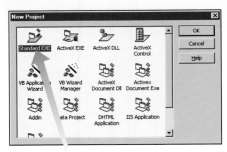

 Click

2 Add a Textbox

Click the **TextBox** control button on the **Toolbox** and place it on the form as shown.

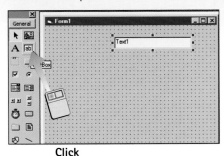

Click

3 Add a Label

Click the **Label** control button on the **Toolbox** and place it on the form as shown.

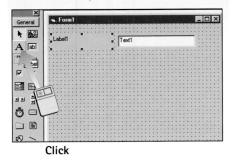

Click

4 Enter Textbox MouseMove Routine

Double-click the textbox to display the **Textbox_Click** routine in the **Code Editor**. Then, select **MouseMove** from the **Procedure** drop-down list.

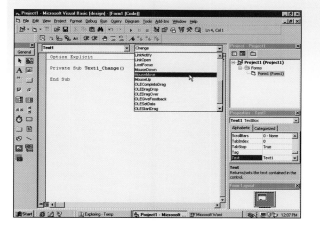

5 Enter Textbox MouseMove Code

Type in the code shown in the **Textbox_MouseMove** routine. By using the **MSGBOX** function, you can display a message when the mouse is placed on the textbox.

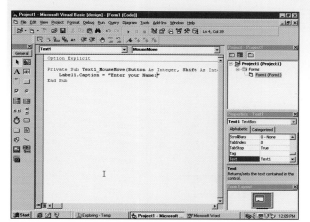

6 Enter Form MouseMove Code

To clear the message from the label when the mouse is not on the textbox, type in the following code in the form's **MouseMove** routine.

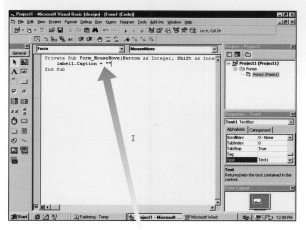

7 Run the Program

To see how this works, click the **Run** button on the Visual Basic **Toolbar** to execute the program and move the mouse over the textbox.

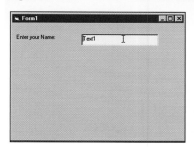

End

How-To Hints

Changing the Mouse Icons

One of the most common actions that is performed using the **MouseMove** event is to change the mouse icon when the mouse is over a given object on the form. This is done by changing the **MousePointer** property.

How to Use the MouseDown Event

Another useful mouse-related event is the **MouseDown** event. This is where you can test to see which mouse button was pressed and which, if any, special key (**Alt**, **Ctrl**, **Shift**) was pressed when the mouse was clicked. This event allows you to associate special processing to each of the mouse buttons. One of the most common uses for the **MouseDown** event is to display a pop-up menu. In this task, you will add two standard menu items and then hide one of them to be used with the **MouseDown** event.

Begin

1 Open the Menu Editor

Display the **Menu Editor** by right-clicking the form and selecting **Menu Editor**.

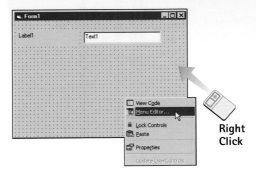

Right Click

2 Create the File Menu

Add a File menu group by adding the **File**, **Open**, **Close**, and **Exit** items, as shown in the editor.

3 Add the Edit Menu

Add an Edit menu group by adding the **Edit**, **Cut**, and **Copy** items, as shown in the editor.

4 Hide the Edit Menu

When using a menu group as a pop-up menu, you must hide it. To do this, select the top of the menu group in the code editor, and then click the **Visible** checkbox property to uncheck it.

5 Add the Form MouseDown Code

MouseDown passes arguments that you can check to see which button was pressed. Enter the code shown in the **Code Editor** to the **MouseDown** routine for the form.

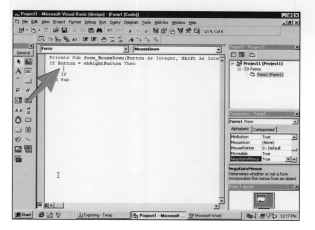

6 Add the Pop-Up Menu Process

The last step is to add the statement to display the pop-up menu when the right mouse button is pressed. This is done with a **PopUpMenu** statement as shown.

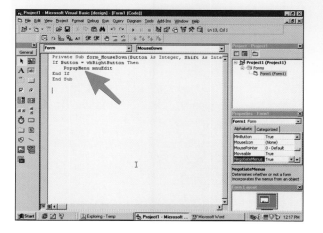

7 Right-Click the Form

To see how all this works, run the program and right-click on the form to display the pop-up menu.

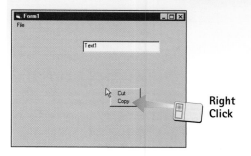

Right Click

End

How-To Hints

Right-Clicking an Input Box

You should be careful when using this technique for an input object such as a textbox. Visual Basic and Windows intercepts the right-click and displays a text edit box before the application gets control.

How to Use the KeyPress Event

Although the objects on a Visual Basic form will automatically recognize any keystrokes and perform the related action, there will be times when you must check to see what key was pressed and take some action before allowing Visual Basic to process the keystroke.

Begin

1 Start a New Project

Start a new project by pulling down the **File** menu and choosing **New**. Then, select **Standard EXE** from the **New Project** dialog and click **OK**.

2 Add a Textbox

Add a textbox to the default form by double-clicking the **TextBox** control button on the **Toolbox**.

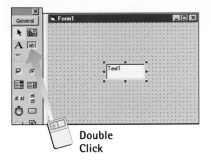

Double Click

3 Display the ASCII Number

Every key on the keyboard has a unique number associated with it. This is called an ASCII number. The **KeyPress** routine accepts the ASCII value of the key that was pressed. To see the value of a key, you can display it using a **MSGBOX** statement as shown in the **Code Editor**.

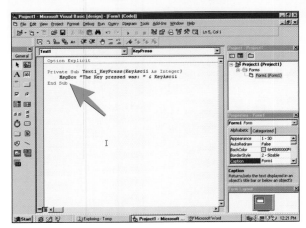

4 Try the Code

Execute the program and type something into the textbox to see how the **KeyPress** routine works.

5 Cancel the Keystroke

When using the **KeyPress** routine to edit any keyboard input, there will be times that you want to cancel the key that was pressed and send a message to the user that he or she typed an invalid character. This is done by setting the **KeyAscii** variable to zero as shown in the **Code Editor**.

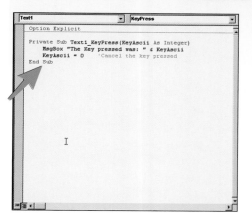

6 Verify the Keystroke

The **KeyPress** routine is generally used to perform some type of edit process against the characters that the user enters. While this can be done after the entire field is entered, there are times when you want to check the input one keystroke at a time. The code shown in the **Code Editor** shows how to check for numeric input and prevent any other key from being entered. If an invalid key is entered, the computer will beep.

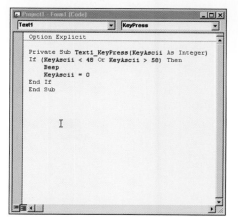

How-To Hints

Keystrokes Not Sent

Although most keystrokes are processed by the **KeyPress** event, there are three important keystrokes that are never sent to it. These are the **Control**, **Shift**, and **Alt** keystrokes. This are processed by Visual Basic and will only be sent to an event routine that requires it.

End

How to Use the KeyDown Event

Even more basic than the **KeyPress** event is the **KeyUp** and **KeyDown** events. These occur whenever the user presses a key and releases a key. This allows you to perform an action based on a key either before Visual Basic is aware of the key being pressed or after the key has been released. This event passes the key code of the key pressed and which special key (**Alt**, **Control**, **Shift**), if any, was pressed.

Begin

1 Check for Special Keys

By checking to see which of the three special keys is being pressed during a **KeyDown** event, you can perform different actions depending on the key pressed. Testing this parameter for each key requires the use of an **AND** condition along with several constants. The **AND** condition will actually check to see if the specified key was hit. The code shown in the **Code Editor** sets a separate value for each key to be used later in the process.

2 Identify a Key Combination

Once you have identified which special keys were pressed, the next step is to test for which standard key was pressed using the **SELECT** statement. The code shown in the **Code Editor** tests for the **F2** key and then for which special key was pressed with it.

3 Start the Key Demo Project

Once you have all of the pieces of the **KeyDown** routine in place, you can use it to process special commands from the user. To see this, place two labels and two textboxes on the default form in a new project, as shown.

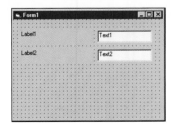

4 Set the KeyPreview Property

In order for the form to be able to identify a key that was pressed before an object like the textbox receives it, you must set the form's **KeyPreview** property to **True**.

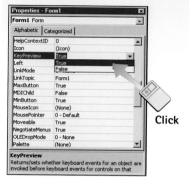

Click

5 Using the KeyDown Routine

The form's **KeyDown** routine will be used to test for the key combinations displayed in the two labels. This will allow the user to move from one textbox to the other by pressing these combinations on the keyboard. The code shown in the **Code Editor** will perform this process. In addition, it will change the background color of the textbox.

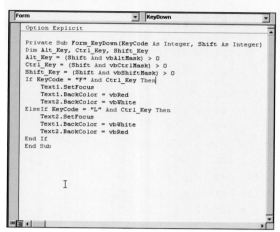

```
Option Explicit

Private Sub Form_KeyDown(KeyCode As Integer, Shift As Integer)
Dim Alt_Key, Ctrl_Key, Shift_Key
Alt_Key = (Shift And vbAltMask) > 0
Ctrl_Key = (Shift And vbCtrlMask) > 0
Shift_Key = (Shift And vbShiftMask) > 0
If KeyCode = "F" And Ctrl_Key Then
    Text1.SetFocus
    Text1.BackColor = vbRed
    Text2.BackColor = vbWhite
ElseIf KeyCode = "L" And Ctrl_Key Then
    Text2.SetFocus
    Text1.BackColor = vbWhite
    Text2.BackColor = vbRed
End If
End Sub
```

6 Test the Routine

Run the program and press the two different key combinations to see how the cursor and focus change from one textbox to the other.

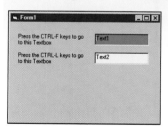

End

How-To Hints

KeyPress

It is important to realize that the three **Key** routines (**KeyDown**, **KeyPress**, **KeyUp**) occur in sequence. Meaning that the **KeyPress** routine will always be executed after the **KeyDown** and before the **KeyUp** routine.

Task

Finding Errors in the Program

There are several types of errors that can be encountered when you create an application. The easy ones are the ones that you can find during development. However, you need to allow your code to handle conditions during runtime that are unexpected during development. For example, your application could be looking for a file that doesn't exist, or your application could attempt to do a write to a full disk. When you develop your application, you need to be able to handle many unforeseen conditions that are not code-related but rather system-related. These are runtime errors and they will cause Visual Basic to terminate your application if you do not intercept them. Of course, while it is difficult to account for each situation, Visual Basic does provide some error-trapping capability.

How to Trap Errors

When you think about trapping errors, you want your code to test for a condition prior to your application aborting. Depending on the type of application, it is always a good idea to test whenever you write code that has the potential to abort—such as database and network connectivity, or file handling.

Begin

1 Using On Error

On Error sets up a condition which enables you to execute a section of code that can avoid the error from terminating your application. For example, if you tried to open a file that didn't exist, you could go to a section of code where the user could create a new file.

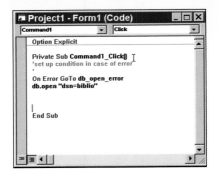

2 Label the GoTo Location

The **GoTo** location in the **On Error** statement is a labeled location. The location must be in the same **Sub** or procedure as the **On Error** condition. The label represents where the code will execute when the **On Error** conditions are encountered.

3 Format Line Labels

The line labels must be unique and a colon must always follow them. This identifies to Visual Basic that it is a label.

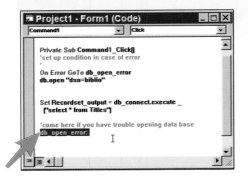

4 Create an Error Message

In this example, you are setting an instruction that the code continue at the statement **db_open_error** when an error is encountered. When the database cannot be opened, you display your own error message rather than the system's and end the code.

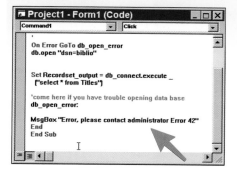

```
On Error GoTo db_open_error
db.open "dsn=biblio"


Set Recordset_output = db_connect.execute _
 ["select * from Titles"]

'come here if you have trouble opening data base
db_open_error:

MsgBox "Error, please contact administrator Error 42"
End
End Sub
```

5 Error Bypass

When Visual Basic executes a **Sub**, it will attempt to process each line. In the case where an error does not exist, you want to exit the procedure prior to the error code execution; for this, you use the **Exit Sub** command. When an error exists, you will go to the line just past the **Exit Sub**.

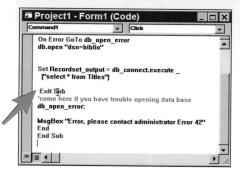

```
On Error GoTo db_open_error
db.open "dsn=biblio"


Set Recordset_output = db_connect.execute _
 ["select * from Titles"]

Exit Sub
'come here if you have trouble opening data base
db_open_error:

MsgBox "Error, please contact administrator Error 42"
End
End Sub
```

End

How-To Hints

Error Condition or State

Since the **On Error** is a state or condition, you do not need to test for each type of error. In the previous example, the error condition would be administered if the database was not found, or if it was corrupt and couldn't be opened.

How to Use the Resume Method

Visual Basic allows you to resume processing rather than exiting after encountering an error. Some errors that the procedure encounters may be correctable and processing could continue. For example, if the user supplied an alpha character and the code tried a numeric operation, the user could simply correct the input.

Begin

1 Using Resume Next

Resume Next will continue processing at the line following the error. This will work for a non-fatal error, where your procedure may continue.

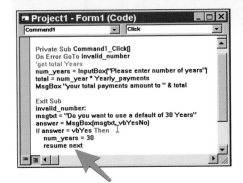

```
Private Sub Command1_Click()
On Error GoTo invalid_number
'get total Years
num_years = InputBox("Please enter number of years")
total = num_year * Yearly_payments
MsgBox "your total payments amount to " & total

Exit Sub
invalid_number:
msgtxt = "Do you want to use a default of 30 Years"
answer = MsgBox(msgtxt, vbYesNo)
If answer = vbYes Then
    num_years = 30
    resume next
```

2 Using Resume

Resume is the best way of handling an error. When you use the **Resume** statement, Visual Basic will simply execute the same line of code where your procedure encountered the error.

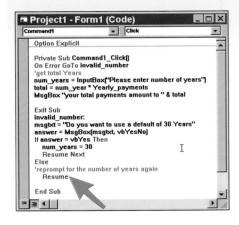

```
Option Explicit

Private Sub Command1_Click()
On Error GoTo invalid_number
'get total Years
num_years = InputBox("Please enter number of years")
total = num_year * Yearly_payments
MsgBox "your total payments amount to " & total

Exit Sub
invalid_number:
msgtxt = "Do you want to use a default of 30 Years"
answer = MsgBox(msgtxt, vbYesNo)
If answer = vbYes Then
    num_years = 30
    Resume Next
Else
'reprompt for the number of years again
    Resume

End Sub
```

3 Using Resume at Label

This method works by sending your code to a new section. The same rules for working with labels apply to the **Resume** as the **On Error** condition. The section where you branch to must be in the same **Sub** or function.

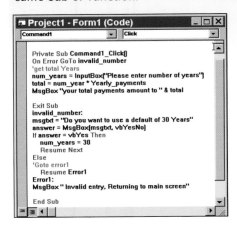

```
Private Sub Command1_Click()
On Error GoTo invalid_number
'get total Years
num_years = InputBox("Please enter number of years")
total = num_year * Yearly_payments
MsgBox "your total payments amount to " & total

Exit Sub
invalid_number:
msgtxt = "Do you want to use a default of 30 Years"
answer = MsgBox(msgtxt, vbYesNo)
If answer = vbYes Then
    num_years = 30
    Resume Next
Else
'Goto error1
    Resume Error1
Error1:
MsgBox " Invalid entry, Returning to main screen"

End Sub
```

4 Using the Exit Method

If you have an application that accesses multiple databases or files, and a file or subsystem is not available, you can choose to exit that section. This will allow the user to continue with other application functionality without ending the application.

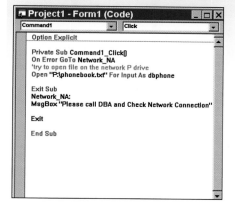

```
Project1 - Form1 (Code)
Command1                    Click
Option Explicit

Private Sub Command1_Click()
On Error GoTo Network_NA
'try to open file on the network P drive
Open "P:\phonebook.txt" For Input As dbphone

Exit Sub
Network_NA:
MsgBox "Please call DBA and Check Network Connection"

Exit

End Sub
```

5 Using the End Method

As you saw in the first part of this section, sometimes there is no way to continue the application. For example, if your database resides on a network that isn't available and your application requires that database, then you use the **End** method to end your application. It is also good practice to display an error message for your user so that he or she will know why the application terminated.

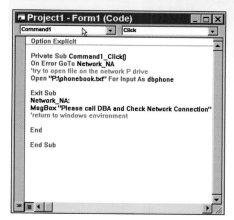

```
Project1 - Form1 (Code)
Command1                    Click
Option Explicit

Private Sub Command1_Click()
On Error GoTo Network_NA
'try to open file on the network P drive
Open "P:\phonebook.txt" For Input As dbphone

Exit Sub
Network_NA:
MsgBox "Please call DBA and Check Network Connection"
'return to windows environment

End

End Sub
```

End

How-To Hints

Error End

When you terminate your application due to an error, you can create a unique error message for each occurrence. You can then have an online file to identify the type of error.

How to Use Error Methods

Visual Basic has its own error messages and numbers. These values can be tested and used with your own error-handling procedures.

Begin

1 Using the Err Object

Err is an object in Visual Basic that allows you to determine the values that exist for conditions. This is called **Err** object's **Raise** method, or raising an error. This is useful in determining the exact cause of the error.

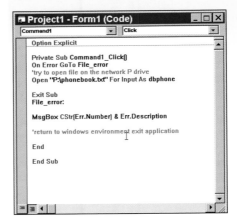

```
Project1 - Form1 (Code)
Command1                    Click
Option Explicit

Private Sub Command1_Click()
On Error GoTo File_error
'try to open file on the network P drive
Open "P:\phonebook.txt" For Input As dbphone

Exit Sub
File_error:

MsgBox CStr(Err.Number) & Err.Description

'return to windows environment exit application

End

End Sub
```

2 Find the Error Number

ErrorNumber is an internal unique number assigned by Visual Basic identifying the error that just occurred.

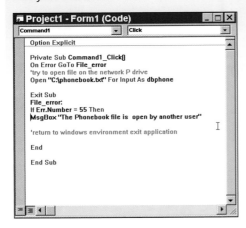

```
Project1 - Form1 (Code)
Command1                    Click
Option Explicit

Private Sub Command1_Click()
On Error GoTo File_error
'try to open file on the network P drive
Open "C:\phonebook.txt" For Input As dbphone

Exit Sub
File_error:
If Err.Number = 55 Then
MsgBox "The Phonebook file is  open by another user"

'return to windows environment exit application

End

End Sub
```

3 Locate the Source and Description

The source contains the current Visual Basic project name. The description contains the Visual Basic error description.

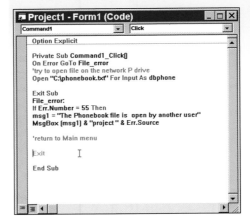

```
Project1 - Form1 (Code)
Command1                    Click
Option Explicit

Private Sub Command1_Click()
On Error GoTo File_error
'try to open file on the network P drive
Open "C:\phonebook.txt" For Input As dbphone

Exit Sub
File_error:
If Err.Number = 55 Then
msg1 = "The Phonebook file is  open by another user"
MsgBox (msg1) & "project " & Err.Source

'return to Main menu

Exit

End Sub
```

4 Test via Code

For some errors that have been discussed, such as file- or hardware-related, you must use Visual Basic's error-handling routines. Other errors, such as user input, can be detected through the use of code that can be written into your program.

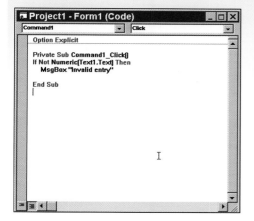

5 Using the Validate Property

Code-writing can be reduced and error-checking can be accomplished using the **Validate** property available with some of the objects.

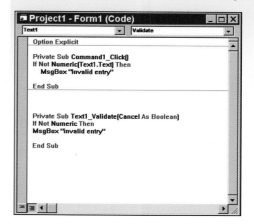

End

How-To Hints

Additional Error Control

Additional error-handling techniques are available through Visual Basic's online help facility. Here, you will see more advanced topics for debugging and dealing with development, as well as runtime errors.

Task

CHAPTER 12

How to Find Problems in the Program

Whenever you create a new application or modify an existing one, there will usually be problems. The way that you remove these problems is by testing the application. By testing, the problems hopefully will show themselves. The process by which you find these problems is called debugging. This is a two-part process that includes determining what the problem is and its location in the program code, and then of course fixing it.

The Windows environment itself has an effect on the testing process. Because both Visual Basic and Windows are interactive, the debugging process is a lot shorter than it could be. The reason is that when an application has a bug, Visual Basic stops the execution of the application with an error message. These are the easy bugs to fix because the program stops at the statement with the problem. However, there is another group of problems that are not as simple to find— when the program runs to completion, but provides incorrect answers. To find these, you must go through the program code one line at a time to find the problem. This chapter shows you how to use the debugging tools provided by Visual Basic to find problems in the code. ●

How to Step Through a Program

The best way to find errors in the program code is to execute the code one line at a time. The Visual Basic debugging environment provides you with several different ways of doing this. Single-stepping and breakpoints give you the control on the program execution that you need to debug your application. Breakpoints allow you to tell Visual Basic to stop the execution of the program when it hits the statement with the breakpoint set on it.

Begin

1 Set a Breakpoint

To set a breakpoint, locate the line of code you want to stop at and click in the left margin. Another way to set a breakpoint is to select the statement and press the **F9** key. This will change the color of the line indicating that a breakpoint is set.

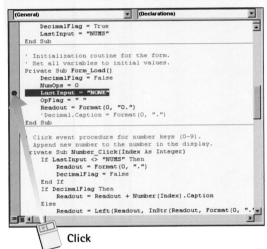

Click

2 Use the Breakpoint

Start the program and perform the action that will execute the code you are testing. The program will stop at the statement with the breakpoint.

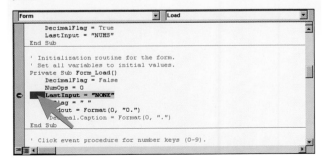

3 Single-Step the Code

From this point, you can single-step, or execute, one line of code at a time by simply hitting the **F8** key. This allows you to see how the logic of the program is executed.

4 Execute Sections of Code

If you want to skip a section of the code, you can place the cursor where you want to stop and choose **Run To Cursor** from the **Debug** menu.

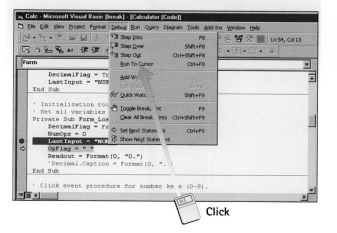

Click

5 Set the Next Statement to

When the program is stopped, you can specify the next statement to be executed by clicking that statement and choosing **Set Next Statement** from the **Debug** menu.

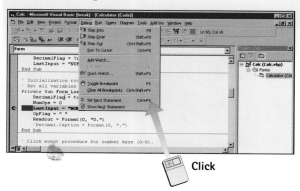

Click

6 Use the ToolTip Display

When your program is stopped, you can display the value of a variable by placing the mouse on the variable.

End

How-To Hints

Breakpoints

Using breakpoints to stop at a particular statement enables you to check the values of the data as the process is being performed.

Single-Stepping

The best way to know if the program is executing correctly is to follow the logic flow using the single-step options.

How to Use the Immediate Window

The **Immediate window** can be used whenever the program has been paused either at a breakpoint or when single-stepping. It allows you to execute any valid Visual Basic statement. The **Immediate window** allows you to change the values of the variables in your program giving you the chance to test for conditions that are very hard to produce normally.

Begin

1 Display Variable Information

To display any variable, property, or calculation, you would simply use the **Print** statement or "?" character, which will also print what follows it.

2 Check an Expression

You can also check the result of a Boolean expression to see whether an **IF** statement will be processed by printing the expression to notice if it is **True** or **False**.

3 Modify the Value of a Variable

During the testing process, you might need to change a value in a variable or property to see what the program will do.

4 Print Variable Data

The **Immediate window** is also used by the **Debug** object when the **Print** method is executed. This allows you to print information as the program executes without stopping.

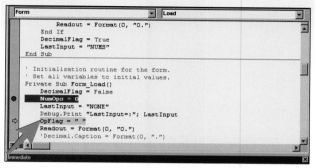

```
                  Readout = Format(0, "0.")
          End If
          DecimalFlag = True
          LastInput = "NUMS"
End Sub

' Initialization routine for the form.
' Set all variables to initial values.
Private Sub Form_Load()
          DecimalFlag = False
          NumOps = 0
          LastInput = "NONE"
          Debug.Print "LastInput=:"; LastInput
          OpFlag = " "
          Readout = Format(0, "0.")
          'Decimal.Caption = Format(0, ".")
```

End

How-To Hints

Debug.Print

In order for the **Immediate window** to be used properly with the **Debug.Print** method, you must set a breakpoint in the program before it finishes execution. If the program ends, you will not be able to see the information printed in the **Immediate window**.

Changing Variable Values

If you are changing a value to test a condition in the program, you should do this before the section of code is executed. If it is already executed or you are at a breakpoint within the section, you must remember to set the **Next** statement to **Execute**. Otherwise, the change might not be used.

How to Use the Watch Expression

There are times when you want to stop the execution of the program only when a value or expression changes. In addition, you might want to see how certain values change as the program is executed. This is all done using watch expressions.

Begin

1 Add a Watch Expression

To add a watch expression on a variable, right-click the variable and choose **Add Watch** from the pop-up menu.

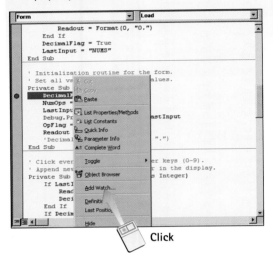

Click

2 Specify the Variable Name

Once you select the variable and open the **Watch** dialog, the name of the variable is placed in the **Expression** textbox.

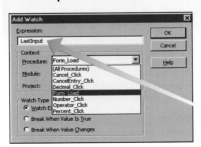

3 Set the Scope of the Expression

Choose where you want the watch expression to be active using both the **Context Procedure** and **Context Module** drop-down lists.

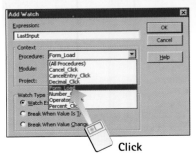

Click

4 Specify a Break or Watch

Finally, you can either watch the expression as it changes or have the program stop or break when it does change.

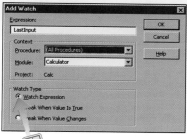

 Click

5 Identify the Expression Type

For each of the different watch types, there is a unique icon used on the **Watch** window to distinguish them.

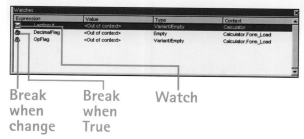

Break when change

Break when True

Watch

End

How-To Hints

Using a Watch properly

There will be times when debugging your application code that you will need to find where a particular variable is being changed. This is done using a watch expression that stops whenever the variable's value is changed. This will pinpoint where in the application this is happening. In fact, by setting an expression, you can stop only when the variable contains a specific value.

Task

13

Using Standard Controls

*C*ontrols allow you to create your interface windows. You can include controls that allow the user to maneuver through the application. Buttons on the **Toolbox**, which allow you to paint your window, represent controls. When you click a control, you are selecting that control to paint. You then click and drag on the form where you want the control placed. Double-clicking a control places the control in the center of your window. Properties control the behavior of the objects. Although you have used some of these controls in previous examples, this chapter reviews how the properties affect the controls, and how to use them. ●

How to Use the TextBox Control

Visual Basic comes with many controls; the standard controls appear in your **Toolbox** when you start Visual Basic. Visual Basic provides the capability of adding additional controls to your **Toolbox**. The standard controls are the most frequently used and appear in most applications. A textbox is an area where users can display or capture data. The data can be used to update information in a database or be used as information data by the application.

Begin

1 Using the Alignment Property

The **Alignment** property allows you to determine the justification of the text in the textbox. The default value is **Left Justify**, with options for **Center** and **Right Justify**. The options are available through a drop-down list in the **Properties window**.

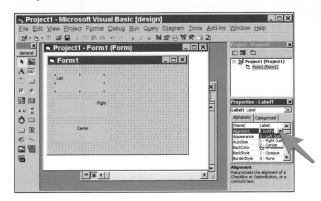

2 Using the PasswordChar Property

The **PasswordChar** property is used to protect the textbox. You select a character; that character is displayed as the user enters information. This is particularly good for a password prompt.

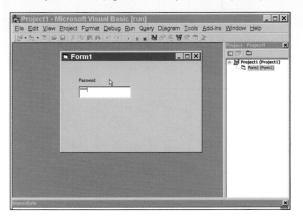

3 Using the MaxLength Property

The TextBox control can handle thousands of characters in the **Text** property. The **MaxLength** property will limit the number of available characters that the **Text** property will handle.

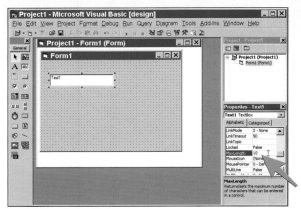

4 Using the MultiLine Property

In the default state, the **Text** property will not accept a carriage return; it will, however, keep accepting information and scroll out of the textbox range. The **MultiLine** property will allow your user to enter multiple lines of text.

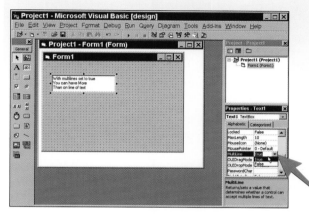

5 Using the ScrollBars Property

The **ScrollBars** property has several options available—**None**, **Horizontal**, **Vertical**, or **Both**. When used in conjunction with **MultiLine**, it creates scrollbars associated with the textbox that allow the user to scroll through the text.

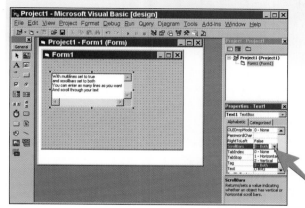

6 Using Height and Width Properties

Height and **Width** are numeric value properties that determine the height and width of your object. When you resize your object using your mouse, you can see that the property values change.

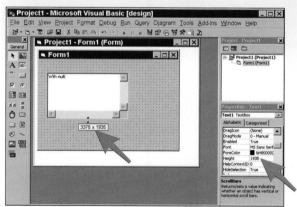

7 Using CausesValidation Property

This is a new feature for Visual Basic 6. When **CausesValidation** is set to **True**, it will automatically apply the validation test that has been coded for the **Validate** event.

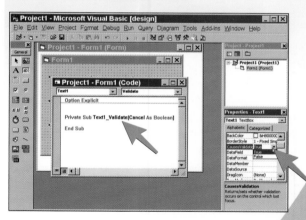

End

How to Use Program Controls

The Label control allows you to create descriptive text on your form. When you combine the Label control with the TextBox control, you can essentially create an online form. In fact, the two controls are very similar; the major difference is that the Label control is used for information only. It will not accept input from the user.

Another such control, which the user does not even see, is the Timer control. This control is used to create a timed or delay mechanism for your code. It will cause a delay in the execution of your code for a specified time interval.

Begin

1 Using the Visible Property

The **Visible** property is a **True/False** value that determines whether the object is visible or hidden. You can choose to leave a label hidden and then display it through code, based on provided information.

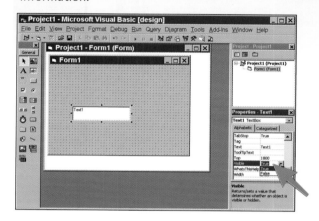

2 Using the UseMnemonic Property

The **UseMnemonic** property controls how Visual Basic treats the ampersand key (&). When **UseMnemonic** is set to **True**, the ampersand will underline the next character. When it is set to **False**, the ampersand will be a printed character.

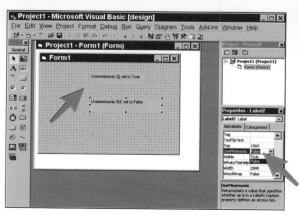

3 Using the AutoSize Property

AutoSize will automatically size your label to fit the text entered. If you redefined your text using the Label control's **Caption** property in your code, the Label control size will change.

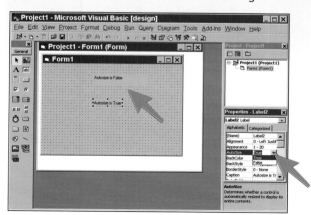

4 Using the Timer Control

The **Timer** control button is the icon that looks like a stopwatch. When you drag it onto your form, it is visible only during design time. When the **Enable** property is set to **True**, it causes the timer event to delay its processing in your application. The delay is specified in the **Interval** property and is represented in milliseconds. Setting the **Interval** value to 5,000 will cause a five-second delay.

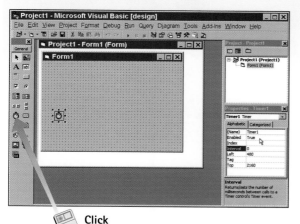

Click

5 Using the Enable Property

The **Enable** property for the timer sets the timer on or off. When **Enable** is set to **True**, that will begin the timer.

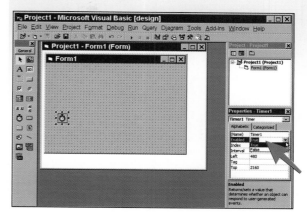

6 Using the Interval Property

The **Interval** property is a value that specifies how long the timer should run. The value of the property is in milliseconds. The maximum delay is approximately one minute.

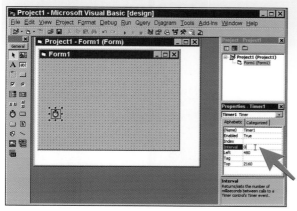

End

How-To Hints

Properties in Common

Most of the properties for the TextBox and the Label controls are shared by both controls. In fact, most of the controls have many common properties.

When Do I Use the Timer?

A functional use for the timer or a delay is during startup; your splash screen might flash across the screen. If you included a delay after showing the splash screen, you could delay the time before it is hidden.

How to Use Selection Controls

When you want your user to provide information that has a limited response, such as marital status, sex, or any information that can be selected and requires no input, Visual Basic provides you with the ability to create a selection option on your form. The CheckBox control creates a box with associated text that the user can toggle on or off. The checkbox is a switch, which will provide a true/false condition.

The OptionButton control is similar to the CheckBox control—it also represents a true/false condition. Option buttons are generally grouped and only one option can be selected. The major difference is that with the CheckBox control, the user may set more than one condition to true.

Begin

1 Using the Value Property

The **Value** property will set the default value. For the CheckBox control, you can select **Checked**, **Unchecked**, or **Grayed**. **Grayed** will be unavailable for the user. For the OptionButton control, it can be **True** (selected) or **False**.

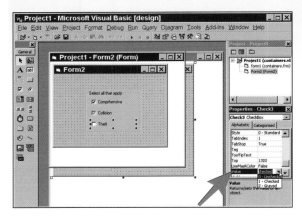

2 Using the Style Property

The **Style** property allows you to choose the appearance of the control. It can be **Standard** or **Graphical**.

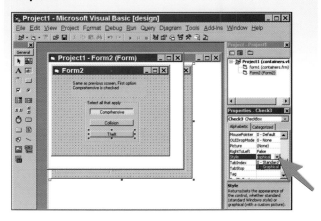

3 Using the Picture Property

If you choose **Graphical** for the **Style** property, you can add a picture to the control with the **Picture** property.

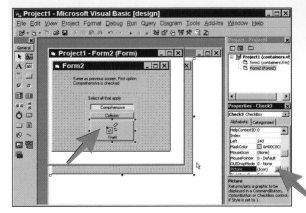

4 Using the MousePointer Property

The **MousePointer** property will change the appearance of your mouse pointer on your control. When you select a different mouse pointer for a control, the pointer will change when you are over that object.

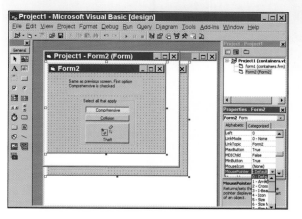

5 Using Group Arrays

When you add a group of option buttons, you can assign them the same name. This will create a group array; using **Select Case** is perfect for option buttons with a group array.

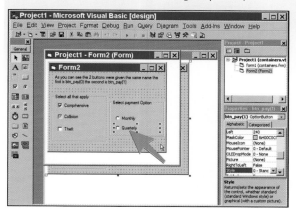

6 Select Options

When you work with checkboxes or option buttons, the use of Booleans is ideal for setting the default criteria for the user's selections.

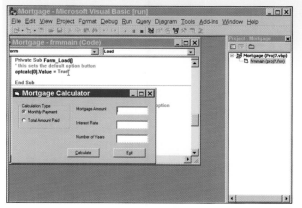

End

How to Use Containers

Containers are unique controls; they allow you to put other controls in them. You use containers for grouping information. You can also use the container to make a group of controls visible or hidden. When using option buttons, you can have several distinct groups on your form. Containers can also be used for producing screens that are easier for your users to work with. This task discusses when containers are required and how to use them to organize your forms.

Begin

1 Using the Frame Control

The Frame control is a container. You can use a frame to group parts of your application together. After you add a frame to your form, you can treat that frame almost as a separate form.

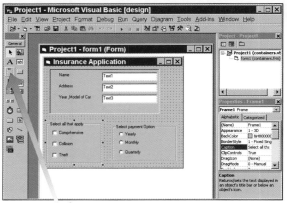

 Click

2 Using the PictureBox Control

The PictureBox control is a container as well. The PictureBox has a **Picture** property that allows you to add a graphics to it. It does not have a **Caption** property to add text.

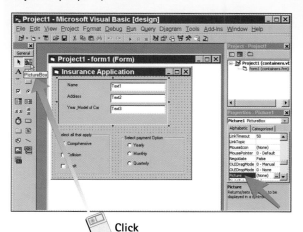

Click

3 Using Groups

Containers are used for organizing groups of data together. This is essential when you want to have multiple groups of option buttons.

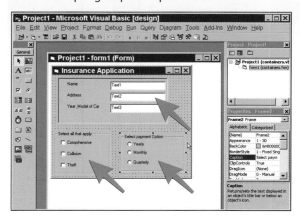

4 Organize Your Screen

You can organize your screen so that similar information can be presented in a container. You could have several containers on a screen.

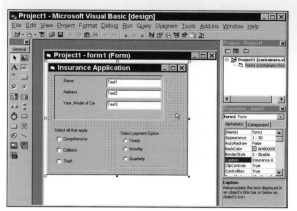

End

How to Use the Format Editor

You have just reviewed how you can incorporate containers in your Visual Basic projects to make them more readable and less busy. You can see how that would keep your forms user-friendly.

You might also want to keep your forms aligned and uniform in terms of font, size, and color. When you work with multiple controls on a form, Visual Basic provides a **Format Editor**. The **Format Editor** allows you to select several objects and apply a change, which will affect them all. Here, you learn how to use the **Format Editor** and what it can be used for.

Begin

1 Select Controls

In order to identify the controls that the **Format Editor** will focus on, you must first select them. There are two basic ways of selecting controls. The first is with your mouse; you click the form and drag the mouse. As you are dragging, you will notice a box appear. Using the box, you lasso all the controls you want to work with. A second option is to click each object, while keeping the **Shift** key depressed.

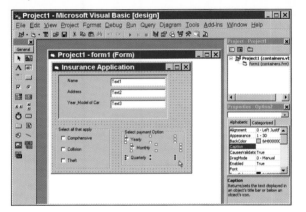

2 Open the Format Menu

After you have your controls selected, click the **Format** menu. You will see options for sizing, alignment, and spacing.

3 Choose the Make Same Size

The **Make Same Size** option allows you to make all your controls the same size. You can select **Width**, **Height**, or **Both**.

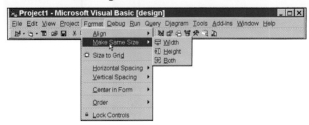

4 Select the Align Option

The **Align** choice allows you to align your controls. The side edges, **Lefts** and **Rights**, can be aligned for vertical controls, and the **Tops** and **Bottoms** for horizontal controls. If you choose to **Align** the **Bottoms** of vertical controls, all the controls will end up on top of each other.

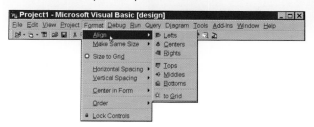

5 Choose a Spacing Option

The spacing choices allow you to determine the spacing between your controls. Here you can **Increase** or **Decrease** the **Vertical** and **Horizontal Spacing**.

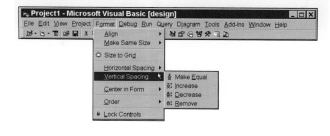

6 Lock Your Controls

When you are in the **Format** menu, you will see a **Lock Controls** option. When you lock your selected controls, you prevent any positional changes to those controls. You cannot move or resize those controls until they are unlocked.

7 Change Properties

While you have your controls selected, you can change the **Font** size or other properties, and the new properties will be in effect for all the selected controls.

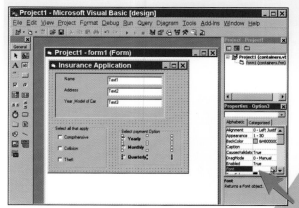

End

How to Use Pictures and Graphics

Because Visual Basic allows you to create a graphical user interface (GUI) application, it stands to reason that pictures and graphics could easily be incorporated into your application. Visual Basic allows the addition of multiple types of graphics and pictures. You can add existing pictures that come with your system or create your own using a paint package or even a scanner. These graphics are intended to jazz up your application. This task reviews adding pictures and graphics to your application.

Begin

1 Using the Shape Control

The Shape control allows you to add several predefined shapes to your form. These include **Rectangle**, **Square**, **Circle**, and **Oval**, chosen through the **Shape** property. Shapes can be used to emphasize an area of your form.

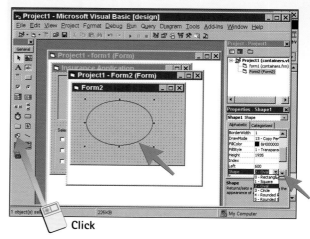

Click

2 Using the Line Control

The Line control enables you to add lines to your form. To draw a line, select the **Line** control button in the **Toolbox**, click the line on the form, and then drag and click to complete the line.

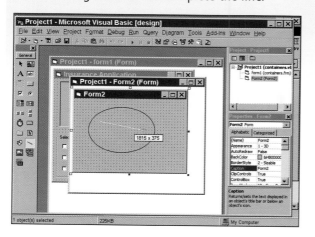

3 Using the BorderStyle Property

The **BorderStyle** property can change the outline of your shape from solids to dots. This property enables you to select a shape to fit your application.

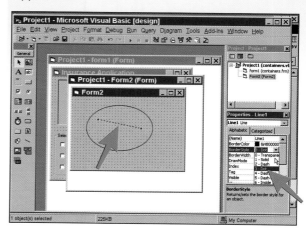

4 Using the BorderWidth Property

To change the width or thickness of the shape outline, use the **BorderWidth** property. When you change the **BorderWidth** property, it will override any changes made in the **BorderStyle** property.

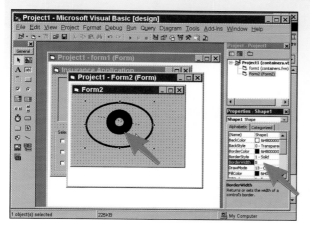

5 Using the Image Control

The Image control allows you to add images directly to your form. Unlike the PictureBox control, which is a container control on the form, the Image control allows you to add an image directly on the form. Visual Basic supports multiple graphic file formats.

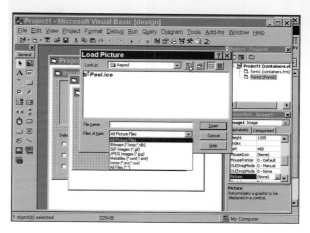

6 Select an Image

When you select the **Picture** property, you will be given a search screen—the **Load Picture** dialog box—to select your image.

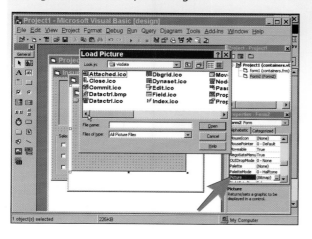

7 Using Added Controls

If your image occupies a large portion of your form, it will act as wallpaper with added controls on top of your image.

End

Task

14

Additional Standard Controls

As you can see from the previously defined controls, they are the visual part of Visual Basic. You will continue to learn the topic of controls and review several other controls. These controls will help enhance your application. ●

How to Use Common Controls

When you open Visual Basic, the **Toolbox** contains controls that are referred to as standard controls. Visual Basic also provides controls that are commonly used by other applications. They are bundled together and called common controls. This task reviews several of these common controls.

Begin

1 Add Common Controls

To add the additional common controls to your **Toolbox**, choose **Components** from the **Project** menu. Select the three available versions of **Microsoft Windows Common Controls**. Click the **OK** button and the controls will be available in your **Toolbox**.

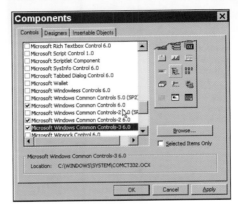

2 Add the Status Bar

The status bar is used to display system information at the bottom of the screen. When you add the status bar to your form, it will occupy the entire width of your form. It contains one panel by default. Each panel within the status bar is an object that contains information.

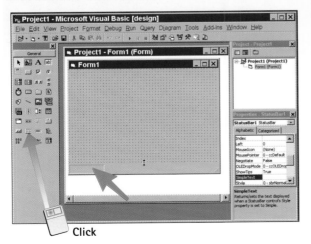

Click

3 Add and Remove Panels

The panels on the status bar can be increased or removed through their properties. To access the property screen, right-click the panel and select **Properties**. Select the **Panels** tab of the **Property Pages**, and you will have the ability to insert or remove panels.

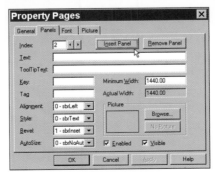

4 Populate Panels

The **Panels** tab also contains a **Style** drop-down box. The available styles are predefined and all start with "sbr" (status bar):

SbrText—Displays user-defined text.

SbrCaps—Displays the status of the **Caps Lock** keyboard button.

SbrScrl—Displays the status of the **Scroll Lock** keyboard button.

SbrNum—Displays the status of the **Number Lock** key.

SbrIns—Display the status of the **Insert** key.

SbrDate—Displays the current date.

SbrTime—Displays the current time.

5 Change Additional Properties

The **Alignment**, **Bevel**, and **AutoSize** properties all affect the visual appearance of the panels. When you change these properties and close the **Property Pages**, you can see the effect on the panel.

6 Change the Text Panel

The text panel will display the text that is defined by you. Set the default **Text** to **Ready**. As you move through your application, you can change the text panel programmatically to keep the users informed as to what the application is doing. As an example, you can change the text to display **Searching For File** to inform the user that the application is busy.

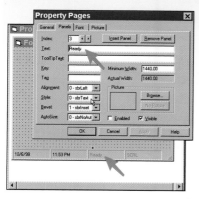

End

How-To Hints

Components

When you add components such as the common controls to your application, the controls will be available the next time you open your project. However when you start a new project, Visual Basic sets up your **Toolbox** only with the standard controls. You need to chose **Project**, **Components** to add the common controls to each project in which you will use them.

How to Use the Progress Bar and Animation Control

You have just seen how to supply your user with information that the application is busy using the sbrText panel. Visual Basic provides additional methods of indicating that the application is busy. The first is the progress bar; it displays the status of the application running while the bar is changing. The second is the Animation control, which plays an AVI video clip while your operation is in progress.

Begin

1 Using the Progress Bar

The progress bar displays how much of an operation has been completed. It also gives the user a good indication of how much additional processing is yet to be done. To add a progress bar to your form, click the **ProgressBar** control button in the **Toolbox**.

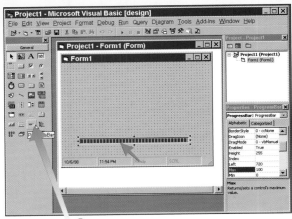

 Click

2 Control the Bar Movement

With the progress bar, you control the **Min** and **Max** values. In your code, you control the movement of the progress bar. The progress bar value will determine the percentage that is filled. For example, if you had 100 files to copy and set the **Min** to 0 and the **Max** to 100, you would increment the value by one each time a file was copied. When the value reached 50, the progress bar would be at fifty percent.

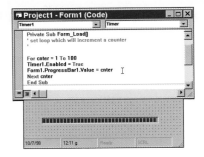

3 Using the Animation Control

The Animation control allows you to add an AVI file to your form. An AVI is a video file to show some action being done, such as the delete process.

4 Display the Animation Control

When the Animation control is added to your form (click the **Animation** control button in the **Toolbox**), it will appear as a box with a movie reel in it representing the location where the AVI will be displayed.

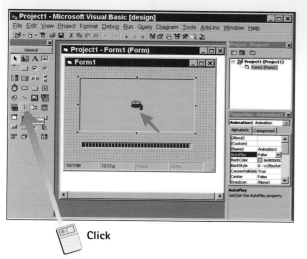

Click

5 Assign an Animation

To assign an animation, the first thing that is required is an AVI file. AVI files that are included with Visual Basic are stored in the Visual Basic subdirectory \Common\graphics\Avis. They are assigned to the Animation control.

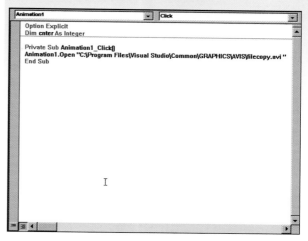

6 Display the Animation

After you assign the AVI, use the **Play** method to display the AVI.

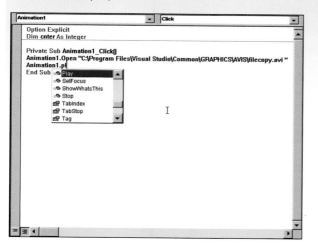

How-To Hints

Busy Applications

You have just reviewed several methods to inform the users that an action is in process. When your application is performing a process that takes a lot of time, it is good practice to show your users that your application is in the midst of processing.

End

How to Use the ListBox Control

The ListBox is a control that creates a box with a list of items that the user can choose from. Items can be added in the **List** property during design time, or the list can be populated programmatically. When the number of items exceed the size of the box, a scrollbar is added automatically. The ListBox control is a standard control that is available when Visual Basic is started. It has multiple options that allow you to control its appearance and behavior.

Begin

1 Populate the Listbox

Entering information into the **List** property will populate the listbox. When you enter your list this way, you need to press the **Ctrl** and **Enter** keys simultaneously to go to a new line. When you press the **Enter** key alone, you will exit the property.

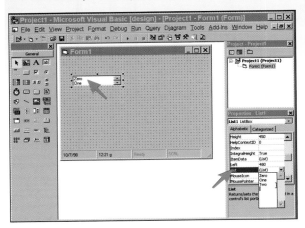

2 Using the AddItem Method

To populate the list box using code, you use the **AddItem** method. This can be incorporated to read text files that can then be displayed as items in the listbox. To clear the contents, you use the **Clear** method.

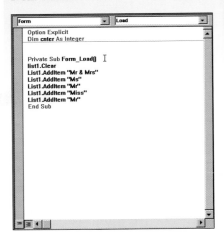

3 Arrange Selected Items

The items populated in a listbox are arranged using **ListIndex**. The **ListIndex** array starts at zero. To determine which item was selected, you would use the **ListIndex** of the list. The following example shows how to get the index value as well as the list value.

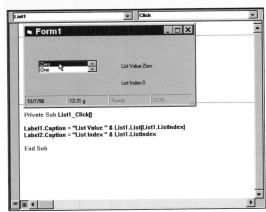

4 Sort Your List

When you want your list sorted, you set the **Sorted** property to **True**. The index value refers to the position in the listbox. As you can see, when the list is sorted, the first value changes but the index remains at zero.

5 Change the Listbox Display

There are several options you can choose to change the display of the listbox. The **Style** property allows you to add a checkbox to your list of options. The **Column** property will generate the list with multiple columns.

6 Using the MultiSelect Property

The **MultiSelect** property will set up conditions where your user can select more than one option from the list. There are basically three options, **None**, **Simple**, and **Extended**:

0 – None—(default) Allows the user to select one option.

1 – Simple—Allows the user to select several options from your list. The user must select or deselect each item separately.

2 – Extended—Allows the user to select multiple items; however, you must use your **Ctrl** key to select more than one item after your initial selection. With **Extended**, your user can use the **Shift** key to select more then one item. For example, if you select the first item and then press the **Shift** key and select the fifth item, all five will be selected.

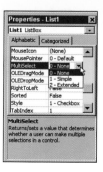

7 Set Up a Loop

When you allow your user to select more then one item from the listbox, you set up a loop to determine which items have been selected. Each indexed item has a **Selected** property, which enables you to test if the item has been selected. In order to use this looping method, you need to know how many items are in your list or the value of the last item, so that you know when to exit the loop.

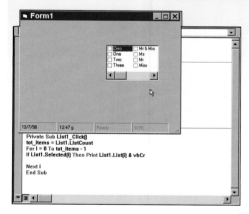

End

How to Use the ComboBox Control

The ComboBox control is similar to the ListBox; they are used for the same purposes—to allow a user to select an option from a list of choices. There are three different types of comboboxes available. The three available types will perform differently; each will, however, save space compared to the listbox. The main distinct difference is that the user can enter information that is not an option on the list. However, the combobox will not allow for multiple item selection. This task reviews the ComboBox control and the similarities to the ListBox control.

Begin

1 Using the Drop-Down List

In the ComboBox control, the drop-down list is **Style** option 0. It is the default and is most similar to the listbox. The user can enter information into the text area, however, the information cannot be added to the list. The drop-down list will have a list of items. It will not be displayed, however, until the user clicks the drop-down pointer.

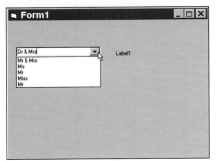

2 Using the Simple Combobox

The simple combobox does not provide a drop-down listing; it offers the user options that can be changed with the use of the arrow keys on the keyboard. You can add the items that the user types in to the existing list. The simple combobox is **Style** option 1.

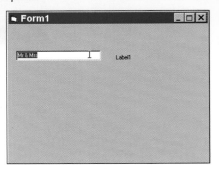

3 Using the Drop-Down Combobox

Style option 2 is a combination of options 0 and 1. The user has the ability to have a drop-down list and view the list of available items. This option does not allow the user to enter items in the text area.

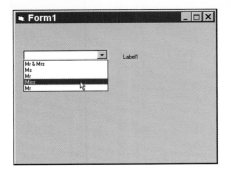

4 Select a Value

The selected value is available to you using the **ListIndex**. You can also use this method to assign the default value of the drop-down text. This is the value that will appear when the screen first appears to the user. You would generally make the default the most commonly selected item.

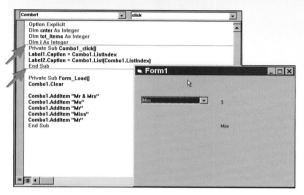

5 Add Items

Using the drop-down or simple drop-down combobox, you can add the items entered by the user to the list. Applying the **Add** method will add items to your list. You must write out the list of options in order to have them available the next time you run your application.

6 Remove Items

Visual Basic also provides the ability to remove items from a list. In order to do so, you use the **RemoveItem** method. This requires that you know the index number of the item you want to delete.

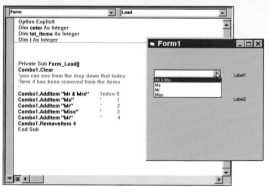

How-To Hints

Adding to Your List

When you want to add items to your list, you need to check that the item doesn't already exist. To save the added items and have them available next time the application is run, you must write out the list items to a file, and read them in next time the application starts.

End

How to Use the ScrollBar Controls

Scrollbars, both horizontal and vertical, provide screen adjustment control. Scrollbars work with assigned values and a **Min** and **Max** capability. You are probably familiar with the use of the scrollbars already. When you are in a word processing document, the scrollbar allows you to move your position within the document. The ScrollBar controls are standard controls. In this chapter, you will see how to work with these controls and review how they function.

Begin

1 Using a ScrollBar Control

The scrollbar has a positioning button that can be dragged to a specific location. It also has left and right arrows that move the position button more slowly. You can also click the bar itself to move in jumps.

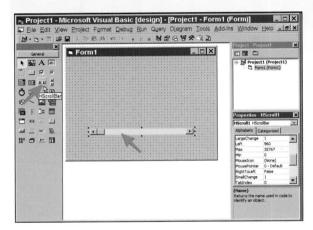

2 Using Value, Max, and Min

The **Value** is the current value based on the position of the scrollbar—this can be set or retrieved. The **Min** value is the lowest value of the **ScrollBar** property. This represents the value when the button is at its leftmost position. The **Max** value is the highest value that it can have and represents the scrollbar value at the rightmost position.

3 Using Alpha Numbers

The scrollbar works with numeric values. When you want to use the scrollbar to display alpha characters, you need to convert them using the **ASC** (ASCII) function. To convert back, you need to use the **CHR$** (Character) function.

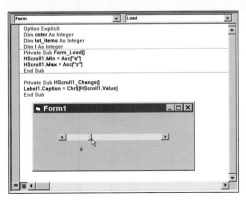

CHAPTER 14: ADDITIONAL STANDARD CONTROLS

4 Change a Property

The ScrollBar controls have a **SmallChange** and a **LargeChange** property; these properties control the speed at which the value of the scrollbar changes. **SmallChange** is assigned to the arrow click, whereas **LargeChange** is assigned to the jumps when you click the bar.

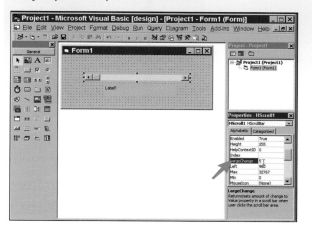

5 Set Visible Values

The scrollbar does not have any default view of what its value is. In order to give the user the exact value of the location in the scrollbar, you must display the value in a Label control.

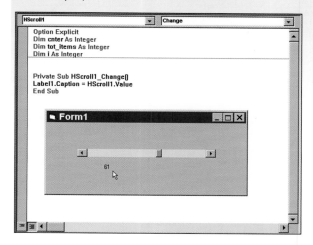

6 Code the Events

In order to keep the value changing, you need to add code to two separate events—the **Change** event and the **Scroll** event. **Change** will be used when the scrolls are used; the other when the bar is clicked.

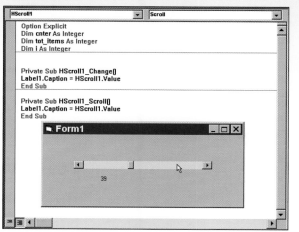

How-To Hints

ScrollBar Controls

You may be wondering how these controls can be utilized. You have probably seen them used to control your position in a document or as a volume control within your Windows software. You could also allow your user to scroll to a position in a database.

End

How to Use the UpDown and Slider Controls

Visual Basic provides additional controls—UpDown and Slider—with the same functionality as the ScrollBar, which allows you to assign values. Both controls are found in the common controls. The UpDown control is used in conjunction with other controls. The Slider control provides a mechanism for users to supply numeric data using a graphical interface.

Begin

1 Using the UpDown Control

To add the UpDown control to your form, click the **UpDown** control button in the **Toolbox**. The UpDown control requires another control to function with, such as a Label or TextBox control. The controls are connected using the **BuddyControl** property.

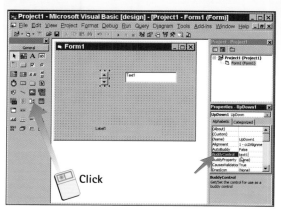

Click

2 Change the Control's Appearance

The UpDown control has two properties that affect its appearance—**Alignment** and **Orientation**. The **Alignment** property determines on which side of the buddy control the UpDown control will appear. **Orientation** determines whether the control itself will function with vertical or horizontal arrows.

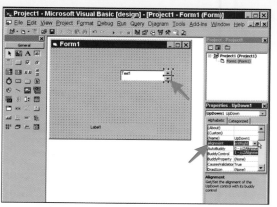

3 Determine Values

The UpDown control has **Max** and **Min** properties, which are used the same way you would use them for the scrollbars. However, the value that is selected by the user is determined by its buddy control.

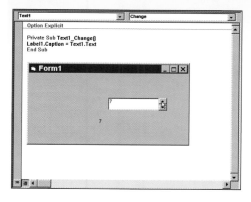

4 Using the Slider Control

Click the **Slider** control button in the **Toolbox** to place the control on your form. The Slider control is, again, similar in functioning to the controls already discussed. This control, however, displays its value as you move the slider, or when you click the slider. You can choose to display this horizontally or vertically.

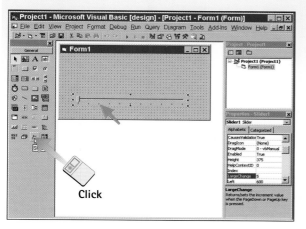

Click

5 Using the TickStyle Property

The Slider control has marks associated to the control; the **TickStyle** property changes how they appear. The value of **0** is bottom or right, **1** is top or left, **2** is tick marks on both sides, and **3** is no tick marks at all.

6 Change Slider Values

The slider has four of the same properties that the scrollbar has—**Max**, **Min**, **LargeChange**, and **SmallChange**. They accomplish the same objectives they have for the scrollbar—control the highest and lowest values and the movement speed.

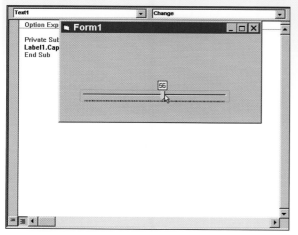

End

Project

For this project, you will experiment with some controls. These exercises will bring up some controls and add some code behind them; however, the real intent is for you to play with the controls and their properties. After you have a control on the form, spend some time with some of the properties to become more confortable with them. Use the online **Help** facility to explore more details about the controls and what the properties do.

1 Start a New Project

Choose **File**, **New Project** from the menu. Select the **Standard EXE** option from the **New** tab of the Visual Basic **New Project** screen. Increase the size of the screen.

2 Select the Common Controls

To open the **Components** dialog, pull down the **Project** menu and choose **Components**. Select the **Microsoft Windows Common Controls** from version 6 in the **Controls** tab. Click **OK**. During or after the exercise project, look at some of the controls that were discussed but you haven't used.

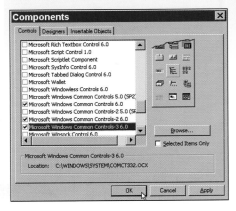

3 Add a Status Bar

Add a status bar to the form by clicking the **StatusBar** control icon in the **Toolbox**. Review some of the properties. Then right-click the control after you have placed it on the form and choose **Properties**.

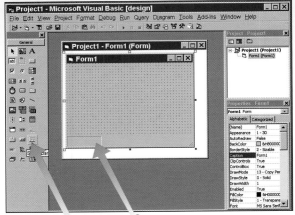

Click   Right Click

4 Insert Panels

Click the **Panels** tab and insert three new panels. Click the down arrow for the **Style**, **Alignment**, and **Bevel** properties' choices. Observe the changes as you change the values.

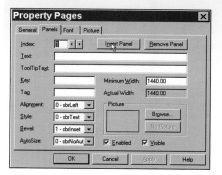

5 Indicate a Text Style

Give the first panel, **Index 1**, a **Style** of **sbrText** and enter **Ready** for the **Text** value.

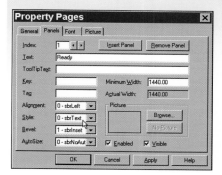

6 Indicate a System Date

For **Index 3**, assign the system date. When you refer to the panels in your code, you use the **Index** value—for example, **Panelname.panel(1)**.

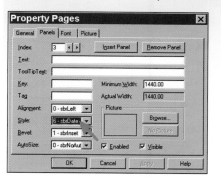

7 Select the System Time

Use the drop-down listbox for the **Style** property and select the system time for **Index 4**.

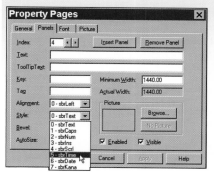

Continues

8 Add a Progress Bar

Draw a progress bar on your form by clicking the **ProgressBar** control button in the **Toolbox**. Assign a **Min** value of **0** and a **Max** value of **1000**. Select title field.

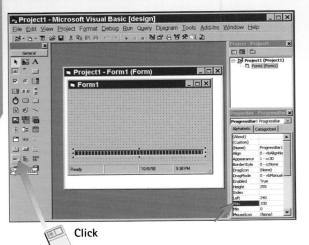

Click

9 Add a Command Button

Add a new command button; **Caption** the button **Try it**. Don't forget to do a quick save of your project.

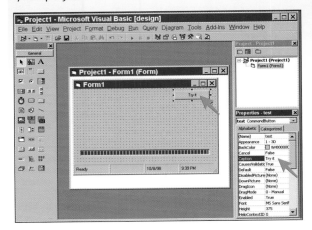

10 Enter Code

Enter the following code and run your application (click the **Start** button). There are several things happening. You are setting the progress bar in a start state, or position 1. You are changing the **Ready** text in the first panel. You then loop and increment the position of the progress bar.

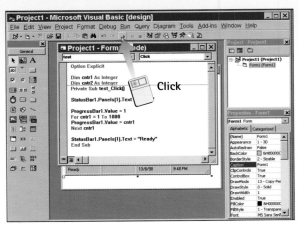

Click

11 Try It

While the code is running, you will see that the progress bar is moving, and the **Ready** text has been changed to **Busy**. When you have completed the loop, Visual Basic resets the text back to **Ready**.

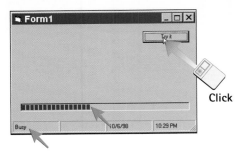

Click

12 Add an Animation Control

Add an Animation control, remembering that you assign an AVI file to the animation. The **Play** method will begin the AVI and **Stop** will stop the AVI.

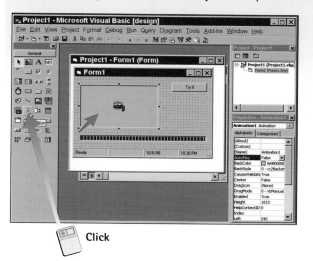

Click

13 Code for Animation

Add the new lines of code to the existing lines. You will find the AVI files in a Common folder in the Visual Basic library. If you are having trouble, use **Find File**.

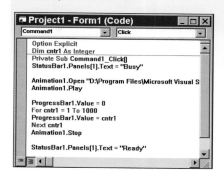

14 Test Run the Application

Run your application. When you click the **Try it** button, the progress bar and the animation will start. Notice that on the screen snapshot, the **Try it** button is covered by the AVI file. You should pay attention to where you place your controls.

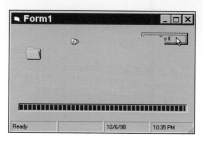

15 Add a Listbox

Remove the Animation control from your screen; don't forget to remove it from your code as well. Add a listbox and two labels to your form.

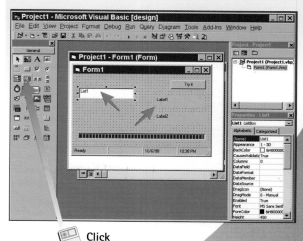

Click

Continues

16 Populate Your List

Add values to the **List** property. Don't forget that for a return, you must have the **Ctrl** key pressed. Enter any values you like.

17 Add More Code

Add the following lines of code. Remember that the first value of your **List** property has an index value of **0**, not **1**. Here you are assigning the **Index** value to `Label1.Caption` and the actual **List** value to `Label2.Caption`.

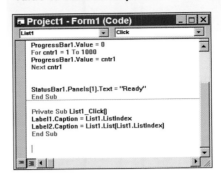

18 Run the Code

Run your application. When you click a value in the listbox, it will display the value and the index in their respective Label controls. Play with the UpDown control and observe the list.

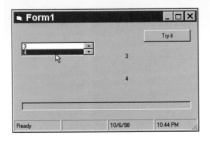

19 Add a New Form

Choose **Project**, **Add Form** to add a new form to the project. Select **Project Properties** from the **Project** menu. Change the **Startup Object** to **Form2**.

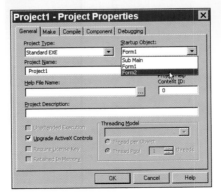

20 Add a Scrollbar

Add the HScrollBar control by clicking the **HScrollBar** control button in the **Toolbox**. You can also experiment with the vertical bar control (VScrollBar). They have the same functionality, just different orientations. Change the **Max** property value to **100**.

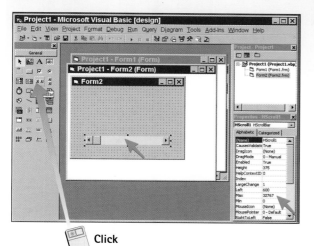

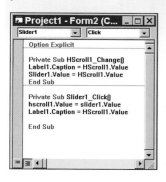 Click

21 Add a Slider Control

Now add a Slider control by clicking the **Slider** control icon in the **Toolbox**. Change the **Max** property value to **100**. As a review, these controls are used for numeric placement or controls based on the location of the button.

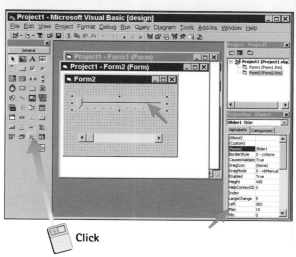

Click

22 Add Even More Code

Add the following lines of code. You have just tied these control values to each other.

```
Option Explicit

Private Sub HScroll1_Change()
Label1.Caption = HScroll1.Value
Slider1.Value = HScroll1.Value
End Sub

Private Sub Slider1_Click()
hscroll1.Value = slider1.Value
Label1.Caption = HScroll1.Value

End Sub
```

23 Run the Application

Run the application, and observe what happens when you move these controls.

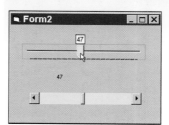

End

Task

15

File System Controls

*U*sers of your application will expect the same easy access to the file system as any commercial application that they are accustomed with. Besides the Common Dialog control, which you will see in Chapter 17, Visual Basic provides three controls that give you the ability to access the drives, folders, and file information within your application. These controls take most of the work out of dealing with selection drives, folders, and files. This allows you to concentrate on the main processing of your application.

For both you and the user of the application, these controls display the file system information much like the ListBox and ComboBox controls that you have seen in Chapter 14. These three controls are included in the **Toolbox** by default, meaning that you do not have to add them to your project before using them. ●

How to List Files

The FileList box is used to allow a user to select a specific file. The FileList box is also smart enough to search the computer and determine which files exist in the file system. It then displays these choices to the user. When the user selects a file, the name of the file is stored in the **FileName** property of the control.

Begin

1 Start a New Project

To start a new project, pull down the **File** menu and choose **New**. Then select the **Standard EXE** project icon and click **OK**.

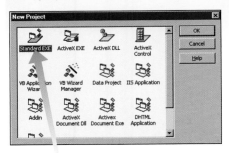

 Click

2 Place the FileList Box on the Form

Click the **FileListBox** control button in the **Toolbox** and draw it on the form as shown.

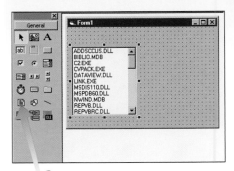

 Click

3 Place a Textbox on the Form

Whenever a file is selected, you should have some way to display it to the user. Click the **Textbox** control button in the **Toolbox** and draw it on the form.

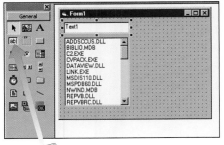

Click

4 Set the Default Path

The FileListBox control displays the files that exist in the current directory path. Using the **CurDir** statement, you can set the current path using the following code in the **Form_Load** routine:

```
File1.Path = CurDir
```

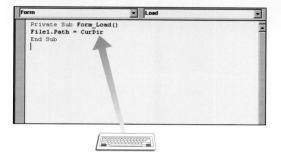

5 Using the Selected File

When a file is selected, the **FileName** property is set to that file. Add the following code to the **File1_Click** routine:

```
Text1.Text = File1.FileName
```

6 Test the Program

Run the application, selecting different files to see how the **Change** routine works.

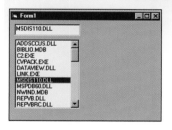

End

How-To Hints

Displaying the Selected File

When using the FileListBox control, you should always display the selected file to the user so that the user can verify that it is the correct file.

How to Use the Folder Control

The Directory listbox is used to allow the user to select a folder from the current drive. The Directory list will search the computer and determine which folders exist on the current hard drive on the computer.

Begin

1 Draw the Directory Control

Using the existing project, click the **DirListBox** control button on the Toolbox and draw it on the form.

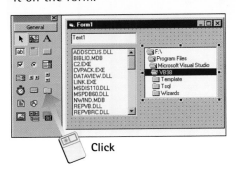

Click

2 Set the Current Directory Path

The DirListBox control will display the folders that exist in the current path. Using the **CurDir** statement, you can set the current path using the following code in the **Form_Load** routine:

```
Dir1.Path = CurDir
```

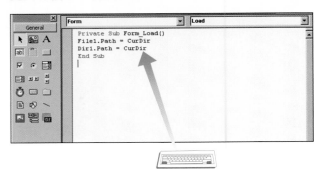

3 Working with the DirListBox

Whenever the user changes the directory, you should also change the **Path** property of the FileListBox control. Add the following code to the **Dir1_Change** routine:

```
File1.Path = Dir1.Path
```

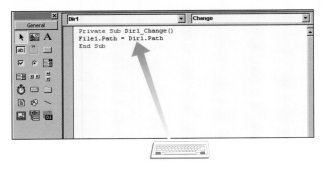

4 Test the Program

Run the application, selecting different folders to see how the **Change** routine affects the FileListBox display.

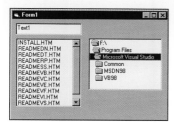

End

How to Display Drive Information

The DriveList box is a drop-down list that displays all of the available drives on the user's computer. Visual Basic will automatically add all the floppy, fixed, and network drives to the list.

Begin

1 Choose the Drive Control

Using the existing project, click the **DriveListBox** control button on the **Toolbox** and draw it on the form.

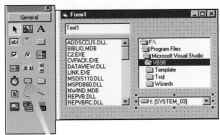

Click

2 Set the Current Drive

The DriveListBox control will display the folders that exist in the current path. Using the **CurDir** statement, you can set the current path using the following code in the **Form_Load** routine:

Drive1.Drive = CurDir

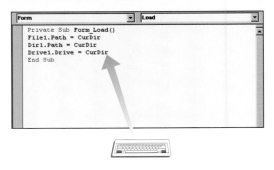

```
Private Sub Form_Load()
    File1.Path = CurDir
    Dir1.Path = CurDir
    Drive1.Drive = CurDir
End Sub
```

3 Working with the DirListBox

Whenever the user changes the drive, you should also change the **Path** property of the DirListBox control. Add the following code to the **Drive1_Change** routine:

Dir1.Path = Drive1.Drive

```
Private Sub Drive1_Change()
    Dir1.Path = Drive1.Drive
End Sub
```

4 Test the Program

Run the application, changing drives to see how the **Change** routine affects both the DirListBox and the FileListBox display.

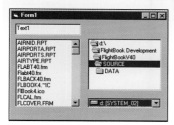

End

How-To Hints

Custom File Selections

These three controls can be used to present the user with a customized file open dialog that includes unique functions related to the application.

Network Drives

The DriveListBox will display any drives that are known to the computer. This includes any drives that are attached to the computer using networking software. This allows you to create an application that is network compatible.

Task

16

Advanced Controls

Visual Basic includes many different types of building blocks that you can use when creating an application. Among the many different controls that come with Visual Basic, there are some that are used which are basic to Windows. In Visual Basic 6, there are many advanced controls that you can use to display data in a new and interesting way. Among these are ways of displaying dates, animation that shows progress or action of some type, and methods of displaying more information on the screen that would normally fit. Finally, there's even a control that allows you to work with documents that include rich text formatting.

While some of these controls have been included with Visual Basic since the first release, others have been added in response to the needs of the users and the complexity of many of the newer applications. Each of the controls described in this chapter displays information to the user in a unique way that the user can easily understand. ●

How to Use the DateTimePicker Control

The DateTimePicker control is used to display the date to the user in a single textbox format. The user can enter the date using the keyboard or by clicking the drop-down arrow to the left of the textbox. This will display a calendar for the current date specified.

Begin

1 Add the DateTimePicker

The DateTimePicker is included in the Microsoft Windows Common Controls-2. To add this to the project, pull down the **Project** menu and choose **Components**.

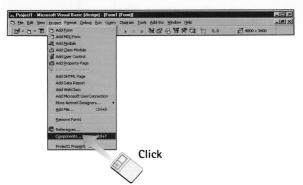

Click

2 Add the Common Controls-2

Locate and select the **Microsoft Windows Common Controls-2 6.0** Control reference and then click the **OK** button to add it to the project.

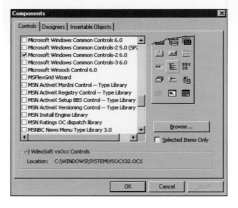

3 Select the DateTimePicker Control

To place the control on the form, double-click the icon in the **Toolbox**. This will place it in the middle of the form. You can then move it where you want it to be.

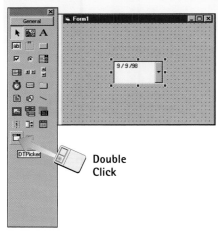

Double Click

4 Set the Current Date

When the DateTimePicker is displayed, it uses the current system date. To change this date, you would set the DateTimePicker's **Value** property using the following code:

```
DTPicker1.Value = Now
```

5 Use the UpDown Buttons

By selecting the **UpDown** option on the **DateTimePicker Property Pages**, you can change the displayed date using the arrows that are displayed.

Click

6 Change the Date Format

The format of the date can be specified by either using the **Format** property drop-down listbox or by specifying a format in the **CustomFormat** property box.

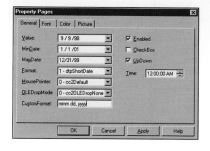

7 Display the Calendar

To display the calendar, the user can click the down arrow in the form.

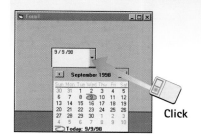

Click

End

How-To Hints

Space

Because the calendar will only appear when needed, the DateTimePicker should be used whenever there is an issue of available space on a form.

Time

If your application requires the user to input a time value, you can use the DateTimePicker to validate the input. The control works with both dates and times.

How to Work with the MonthView Control

If your application requires a little more date information than the DateTimePicker can display, you can use the MonthView control. This control displays one or more months to the user and allows the user to select the date needed. The MonthView control is included in the Microsoft Windows Common Controls-2 along with the DateTimePicker.

Begin

1 Place the MonthView on a Form

The MonthView control requires more space than most controls. To place the control on a form, click the **MonthView** control button on the **Toolbox** and draw it on the form.

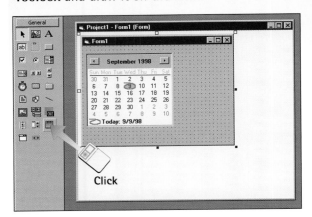

Click

2 Display the MonthView Properties

To display the property page, right-click the **MonthView** control and choose **Properties**.

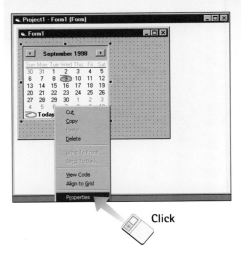

Click

3 Set the Default Date

When the MonthView is displayed, it uses the current system date. To change this date, you would set the MonthView's **Value** property in the property page or in the code using the following statement:

```
MonthView1.Value = Now
```

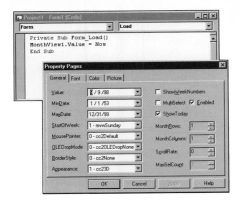

4 Set the Beginning of the Week

Because you are displaying a calendar specifically for your application, you can specify the beginning on the week using the **StartOfWeek** property.

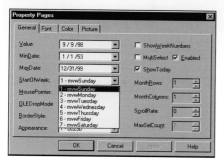

5 Browse the Months

Use the right and left arrows on the MonthView control to navigate from month to month, both forwards and backwards.

6 Change the Month

Another way to change months is to click the current month name to display the drop-down list of months to select from.

7 Changing the Year

When the user clicks the current year displayed, UpDown buttons are displayed. Clicking these buttons will scroll through the years, changing the calendar automatically.

Click

End

_How-To Hints

When to Use MonthView

The MonthView control is very useful in applications where one or more months of a calendar must be visible at all times. This includes applications such as date books or reservation systems.

How to Add Tabs

There are two tab controls that are included with Visual Basic 6. The first tab control is included with the Microsoft Windows Common Control. This is actually a TabStrip control which allows you to display tabs to control what is being displayed on the form. However, the more full-featured control is the Microsoft Tabbed Dialog control. This control allows you to place other controls on each of the tabs independently. When the user clicks a particular tab, only those controls on that tab are displayed automatically.

Begin

1 Add the Tabbed Dialog Control

To add the Tabbed Dialog, pull down the **Project** menu and choose **Components**. Then locate and select the **Microsoft Tabbed Dialog Control 6.0** and click **OK**.

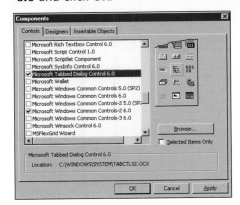

2 Add the Tabbed Dialog

Click the **Tabbed Dialog** button on the **Toolbox** and draw the control on the form.

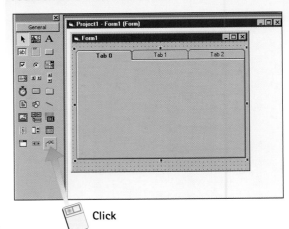

Click

3 Display the Property Pages

To change the properties of the Tabbed Dialog, right-click the control and choose **Properties**.

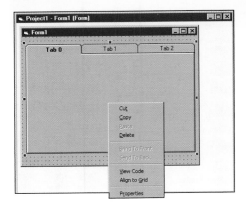

4 Insert Tabs

To add tabs to the dialog, change the value of the **Tab Count** property in the **General** tab.

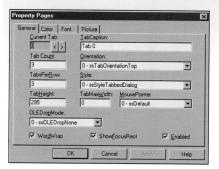

5 Add a Title

To add a title for each tab, select the current tab on the **General** tab and enter a title in the **TabCaption** property.

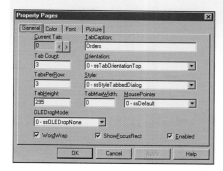

6 Change Tabs

The Tabbed Dialog works much the same way in design mode as it does in run mode. To change from one tab to another, simply click the tab you want to work with.

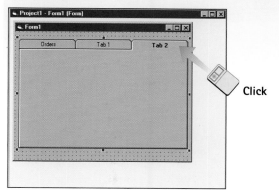

Click

7 Add Other Controls

To add other controls to a tab, select that tab and then add the controls as you would normally.

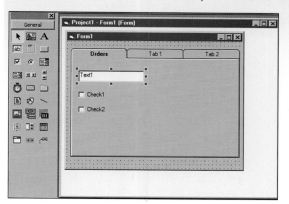

End

How-To Hints

Multiple Tabs

The Tabbed Dialog can be used to create an address book with one "page" or tab per letter in the alphabet. It also lets you logically group your data and display it based on that grouping.

How to Animate Pictures

Another control that is included in the Common Controls-2 set is the Animation control. This control uses special files—called AVI files—to display to the user. An AVI file is actually an animated movie that shows some type of action. You may not know it, but you have seen these in action. Whenever you copy a file in Windows, you see a page floating from one folder to another. This is an animation and you can add it to your application.

Begin

1 Add the Animation Control

Add the Animation control to the form by clicking the **Animation** control button on the **Toolbox** and drawing it on the form.

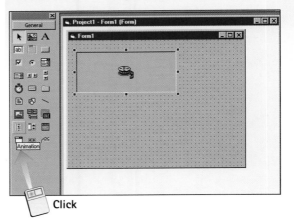

Click

2 Display the Animation Property

To display the **Property Pages**, right-click the **Animation** control and choose **Properties**.

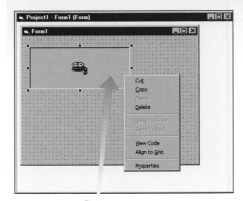

Right Click

3 Set the Properties

The **AutoPlay** property tells Visual Basic to start playing the AVI file immediately when the form with the animation control is shown.

Click

4 Specify the AVI File

To specify the AVI file you want to play, you would pass it as a parameter to the **Open** method of the Animation control. The following code would open the associated file:

```
Animation1.Open "C:\Temp\FileCopy.avi"
```

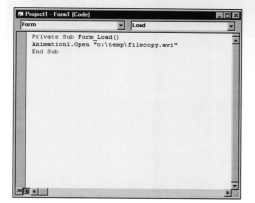

5 Play the Animation

To start the animation on the form, you would either set the **AutoPlay** property to **True**, or you can use the **Play** method using the following code:

```
Animation1.Play
```

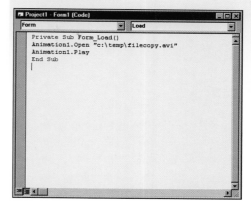

6 Stop the Animation

Once the animation has started, you must issue a command when you want it to stop using the following code:

```
Animation1.Stop
```

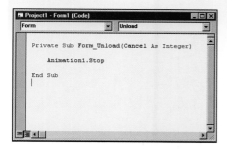

End

How-To Hints

Keeping Busy

One of the most annoying things that an application can do is start a process and give the user no indication that something is actually happening. Using the Animation control provides the user with information about the process.

How to Use the RichTextBox Control

The RichTextBox control provides a number of properties you can use to apply formatting to any portion of text within the control. Using these properties, you can make text bold or italic, change the color, and create superscripts and subscripts.

Begin

1 Include the Control in the Project

To add the RichTextBox control to the project, pull down the **Project** menu and choose **Components**. Then locate the **Microsoft Rich Textbox Control 6.0** and select it.

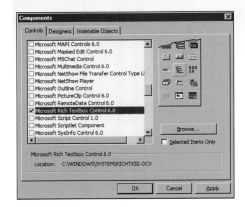

2 Add the RichTextBox Control

Add the RichTextBox control to the form by clicking the **RichTextBox** button on the **Toolbox** and drawing it on the form.

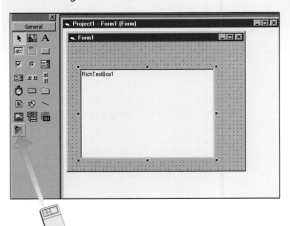

Click

3 Display the RichTextBox

To display the **Property Pages** dialog, right-click the **RichTextBox** control and choose **Properties**.

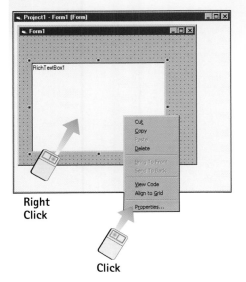

Right
Click

Click

4 Set the Appearance

The **Appearance** tab of the **Property Pages** dialog allows you to change the way the RichTextBox is displayed and whether scrollbars are shown.

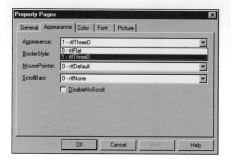

5 Specify the File

The **General** tab allows you to specify the file to load into the RichTextBox control.

6 Use the RichTextBox

Once text is displayed in the RichTextBox, you can modify it the same way you would in any of the more advanced word processors, such as Microsoft Word.

7 Save the Text

To save any text that you may have entered into the RichTextBox control, you would use the **SaveFile** method of the RichTextBox.

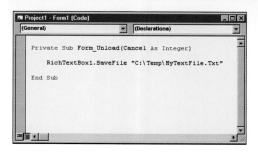

End

Task

CHAPTER 17

The Common Dialog Controls

In most Windows applications, there are several activities or actions that happen frequently. Applications open files, save files, select colors, change fonts, and change printer settings over and over during their work sessions. To make it easier for you to create applications that perform these functions, Visual Basic comes with the Common Dialog control that contains all of the above functions.

Simply adding the Common Dialog control to your application allows you to use its five unique functions in your application. This is done by changing a few properties of the control and executing the method that is related to the function you want to use.

Each of the different functions that are provided by the common dialog do not actually perform any action in your application. For example, when using the **Open** dialog, the Common Dialog control does not actually open the selected file; you must perform that task in your application. The same is true for all of the other functions the control provides. It gives you the information needed to perform the actual process. The tasks in this chapter show you how to use each of the different functions of the Common Dialog control with the minimum amount of code. ●

How to Add the Common Dialog Control

Before you can use any of these functions, you must add the Common Dialog control to the project and then place it on the form. Once the control is on the form, you will have access to all of its many features.

Begin

1 Open the Components Dialog Box

To open the **Components** dialog, pull down the **Project** menu and choose **Components**.

Click

2 Select the Common Dialog Control

Locate and select the **Microsoft Common Dialog Control** reference and then click the **OK** button to add it to the project.

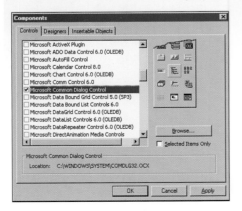

3 Place the Common Dialog Control

To place the control on the form, double-click the icon in the **Toolbox**. This will place it in the middle of the form. You can then move it where you want it to be. The control itself consists of many different forms, but they will not be shown when you add the control.

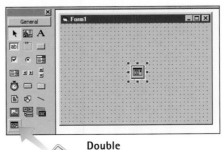

Double Click

4 Display the Properties Dialog

Many of the properties of the common dialog can be set using the **Property Pages** of the control.

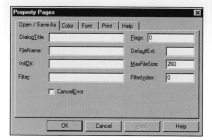

5 Add a Command Button

To see how the Common Dialog control works, you will need a command button to execute the code that will display the common dialog at run-time. Place a command button on the form as shown.

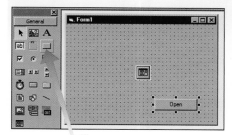

 Click

6 Add a TextBox

When using the **Open** and **Save As** dialog boxes, you will want to see the filename that was selected. The TextBox control gives the program a place to display it. Add a textbox to the form as shown.

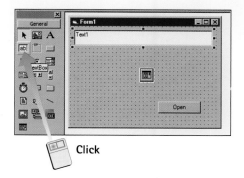

Click

End

How to Use the Open/Save As Dialog Boxes

One of the most common actions that a user will take in an application is the opening and saving of a file. Nearly every application opens at least one file on the hard drive. In applications like Microsoft Word, a user will open and save many different files in a single day. In your application, the user must be able to tell the program what file to open. Then, when they are ready, when and where to save it. Using the Common Dialog control's Open/Save As function gives the user this capability.

Begin

1 Display the Properties Dialog

To display the Common Dialog **Property Pages**, right-click the control and choose **Properties**.

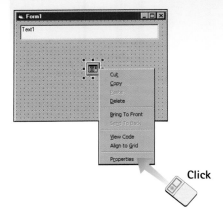

Click

2 Set the Title

The first property to set is **DialogTitle**, which is the title of the dialog when it is displayed.

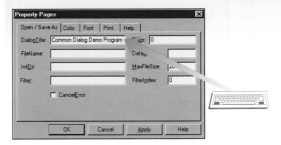

3 Specify the Filter

The **Filter** property tells the common dialog what file types to list when it is displayed. This is done to prevent the user from opening the wrong file.

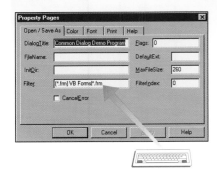

4 Set the Default Extension

When saving a file, the user does not need to specify the extension to use. You can set this default on the **Property Pages** with the **DefaultExt** property.

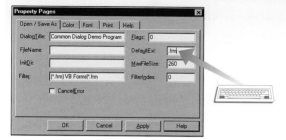

5 Display the Open Dialog

The **Open** dialog is displayed by executing the **ShowOpen** method of the Common Dialog control.

6 Display the Save As Dialog

To display the **Save As** dialog, you would use the **ShowSave** method of the Common Dialog control.

7 Using the File Selected

The **FileName** property contains the file the user selected and can be used to perform the actual task in your application. When the dialog is closed, the filename is placed into the TextBox control.

End

How-To Hints

Using the Filter Property

The **Filter** property is very useful in providing the user of the program with the valid file types that he or she can open or save from the program. This prevents the user from opening a file that is incompatible with the program process.

How to Use the Color Dialog Box

The **Color** dialog is a little different than the other common dialogs in the way it interacts with the user. It gives the user the ability to pick from any color in the spectrum using a **Color** palette. The dialog then passes this information to your application.

Begin

1 Display the Color Properties Dialog

To display the Color **Property Pages**, right-click the common dialog control and choose **Properties**. Then click the **Color** tab.

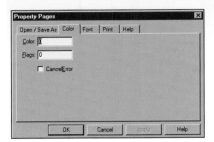

2 Set the Default Color

The **Property Pages** displays only two properties. The **Color** property sets the default or selected color when the dialog is displayed.

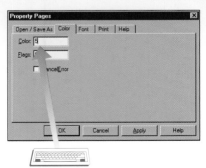

3 Display the Color Dialog

To display the **Color** dialog, use the **ShowColor** method of the Common Dialog control.

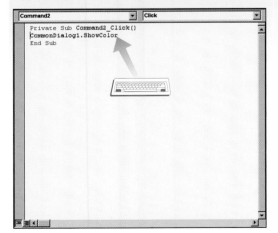

4 Select a Color

The **Color** dialog displays a **Color** palette for you to select a color by clicking it.

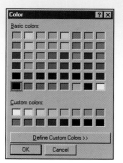

5 Using the Selected Color

The color selected can then be used to change the color of any object in the application. Setting the **BackColor** property of the form after the **Color** dialog is closed will change the form's color.

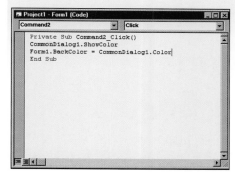

End

How-To Hints

Using Color

Although most Windows applications use the Windows default color scheme, allowing the user to change and set his or her own colors makes the application that much more user-friendly. This means the user can customize the look of the application to his or her own preferences.

How to Use the Font Dialog Box

The capability to change the properties of the text that is displayed in an application can be very useful. It allows the user to highlight certain words, or just make the text easier to read. The **Font** dialog works much the same way as the **Color** dialog, in that it displays the standard **Font** dialog to the user and allows him or her to select the font and its related options.

Begin

1 Display the Font Properties Dialog

To display the **Font** property page, right-click the common dialog control and choose **Properties**. Then click the **Font** tab.

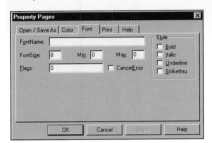

2 Set the Default FontName

The **Property Pages** dialog displays many properties that you should be very familiar with by now. The most important property is the **FontName** property, which is used as the default.

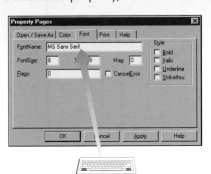

3 Select Font Styles

Setting the **Style** that the user can select can be done from the **Property Pages**; however, it is sometimes easier to use the available constants and set them in the code.

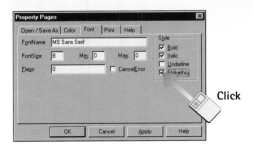

Click

4 Select a Font

The **Font** dialog displays all of the available fonts on your computer for you to select from.

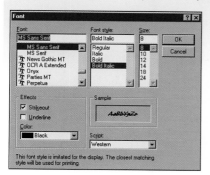

5 Using the Selected Font

The **Font** selected can then be used to change the look of any text in the application. Setting the **Font** property of the textbox after the **Font** dialog is closed will change the font style.

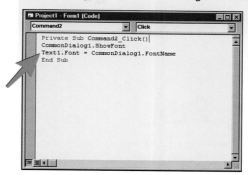

End

How-To Hints

Using Fonts

The **Font** dialog can be used to allow the user to change any of the text displays in the application. This allows the user to make text easier to read than with the standard fonts that are used.

How to Use the Printer Dialog Box

If you have worked with any Windows application, you are probably very familiar with the **Printer** dialog. This dialog allows you to select the printer to use, as well as other options that affect the printing of a file.

Begin

1 Display the Printer Properties Dialog

To display the Printer **Property Pages**, right-click the common dialog control and choose **Properties**. Then click the **Print** tab.

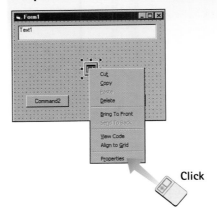

Click

2 Set the Printer Properties

The Print **Property Pages** dialog displays many properties that you can set for the printer.

3 Select a Printer

The **Print** dialog displays the **Name** of all the available printers in a drop-down list to select from.

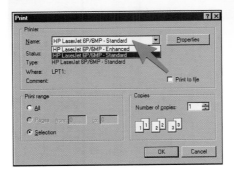

4 Set Printer Options

When the **Print** dialog is displayed using the **ShowPrinter** method, the print **Properties** that can be changed are immediately available to your Visual Basic program.

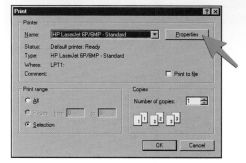

5 Set the PrinterDefault Property

When using the **Print** dialog, you can allow the user to change the properties for the default printer by clicking the **PrinterDefault** checkbox. When the **PrinterDefault** checkbox is checked, any changes made by the user will affect the default printer.

Click

End

How-To Hints

Printer Selection

Although most computers have only one printer installed, there is always a chance that more than one print driver is available on the computer (such as Fax, Printer). The **Print** dialog allows the user to choose the one they want and change the options before printing the information.

Project

When creating an application that requires the user to open and save files, change fonts, and maybe change the colors of the application, the common dialog becomes useful. The Common Dialog control gives you the tools to present the user with standard dialogs from which they can change these properties. This project will teach you to create a simple application that uses several controls besides the Common Dialog control, showing you how the Common Dialog control interacts with these other controls in your application.

1 Start a New Project

In Visual Basic, pull down the **File** menu and choose **New Project**. This will display the **New Project** dialog box.

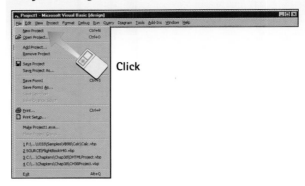

Click

2 Select the Standard EXE Project

Select the **Standard EXE** from the **New Project** dialog and click the **OK** button.

3 Display the Components Dialog

Pull down the **Project** menu and choose **Components**. This will display the **Components** dialog, which is used to add additional controls to the project.

Click

4 Add the Common Dialog Control

Find the **Microsoft Common Dialog Control 6.0** entry in the list and click the checkbox to select it and add it to your Visual Basic project.

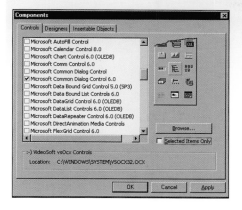

5 Add the Rich Textbox Control

Find the **Microsoft Rich Textbox Control 6.0** entry in the list and click the checkbox to select it. Then click **OK** to add it to the project.

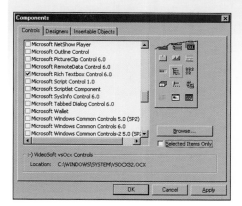

6 Place the Common Dialog Control

Double-click the **Common Dialog** control button in the **Toolbox** to add it to the form.

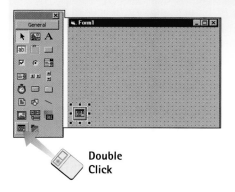

Double Click

7 Add the Open Command Button

Place a command button on the form, changing the **Caption** property to **&Open** and the **Name** property to **cmdOpen**. This button will be used to display the **Open** common dialog.

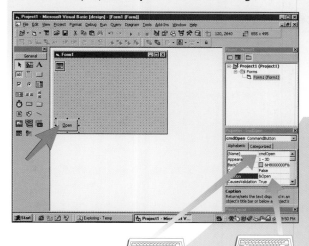

Continues

8 Add the Save Command Button

Place a command button on the form, changing the **Caption** property to **&Save** and the **Name** property to **cmdSave**. This button will be used to display the **Save** common dialog.

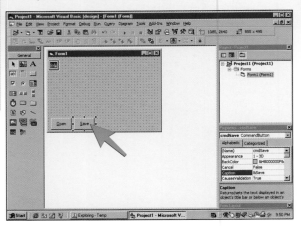

9 Add the Exit Command Button

Place a command button on the form, changing the **Caption** property to **&Exit** and the **Name** property to **cmdExit**.

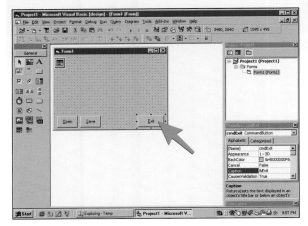

10 Add the Print Command Button

Place a command button on the form, changing the **Caption** property to **&Print** and the **Name** property to **cmdPrint**. This button will be used to display the **Print** common dialog.

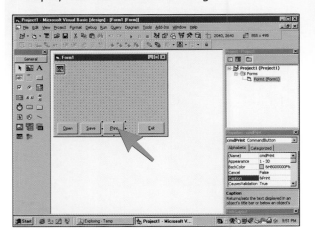

11 Place the Rich TextBox Control

The Rich TextBox control is used to display the text from a file that the project has opened. To add the control to the form, click the **Rich TextBox** control button in the **Toolbox** and draw it on the form as shown.

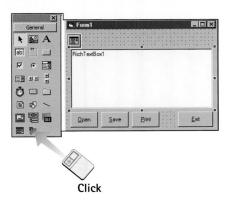

Click

12 Open the Menu Editor

With the form displayed, click the **Menu Editor** button on the Visual Basic **Toolbar**.

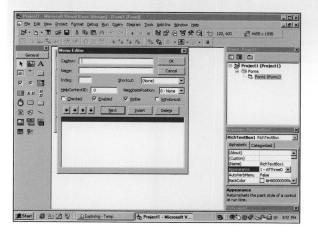

13 Add a Menu to the Form

Add the following items (File, Edit) as shown using the File item as the example.

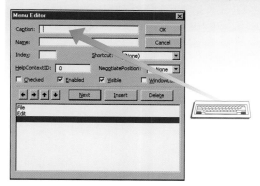

14 Add the File Menu Subitems

For the File menu, add the following items to its second level (Open, Close, Save, Print, Exit) as shown.

15 Add the Edit Menu Subitems

For the Edit menu, add the following items to its second level (Add Font) as shown.

Continues

16 Add the Exit Code

Add the **End** statement to the **cmdExit_Click** routine.

17 Add the Open Code

Add the code shown to the **cmdOpen_Click** routine to display the **Open** common dialog.

18 Add the Close/Save Code

Add the code shown to the **cmdSave_Click** routine to display the **Save** common dialog.

19 Add the Font Code

Add the code shown to the **mnuEFont_Click** routine to display the **Font** common dialog.

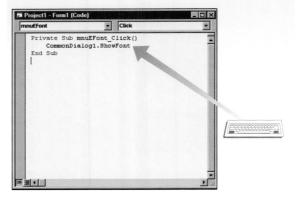

20 Add the Print Code

Add the code shown to the **cmdPrint_Click** routine to display the **Print** common dialog.

```
Private Sub cmdPrint_Click()
    CommonDialog1.ShowPrinter
End Sub
```

21 Run the Application

Run the application and open a file to see how the text in the file is displayed in the rich textbox.

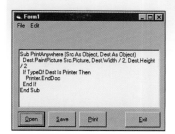

End

Task

CHAPTER 18

Working with Simple Files

Almost every program used today reads and/or writes data to some type of file. This enables the program to save information that it uses and then retrieves later. Whereas most sophisticated applications make use of database processing, some still use simple files to process information.

Several commands in Visual Basic are common to all forms of file input and output. These commands open the file, specify how the file is to be accessed, close the file, and check for free file numbers to be used. When you are finished with this chapter, you will understand how to open a file, read data from it, write data to it, and close it when you are done with it. ●

How to Use the Open Statement

The **Open** statement starts a channel for reading and/or writing to a file. After the channel is open, the data stream can flow. The **Open** statement must include the filename and channel number. The remaining parameters are optional and are used to specify how the file is used.

Begin

1 Open a File for Output

Opening a file in Visual Basic for output requires the use of the **Open** statement while specifying the **Output** parameter.

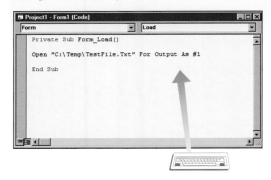

2 Open a File for Input

Changing the **For** option of the **Open** statement to **Input** enables you to read information from a file.

3 Append to the File

If you need to write data to the file but keep any existing data, use the **For Append** option in the **Open** statement.

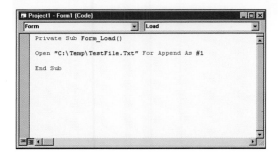

4 Open a Random File

To read or write any record in a file directly, use the **For Random** option of the **Open** statement.

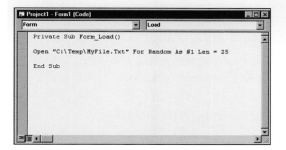

5 Open a Binary File

If your program requires the capability to read or write data in a file one or more bytes or characters at a time, open that file using the **For Binary** option of the **Open** statement.

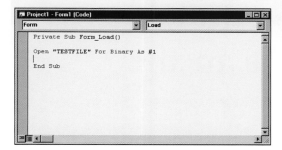

6 Using the FreeFile Function

The **FreeFile** function is used to determine the next available channel number that you can use in your program. This function prevents errors from occurring in your program because it prevents you from using a channel number that is already in use.

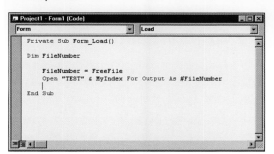

7 Close the File

All files that were opened using the **Open** statement need to be closed. If a channel number is specified with the **Close** keyword, only the file opened with that number is closed.

End

How-To Hints

Simple File I/O

Using simple files within a Visual Basic application gives you the ability to read and write data without having to interface with larger, more complicated database systems. However, the capabilities of these files are completely reliant on your program code.

How to Write Data to the File

Opening is the first step required to use a file. After the file is open, you must have some way of putting data into it. Visual Basic provides several commands to enable you to do this. The commands are specific to the type of file you are opening.

Begin

1 Start a New Project

Choose **New** from the **File** menu, select **Standard EXE** from the **New Project** dialog, and click **OK**.

 Click

2 Add a Textbox

To see how data in a file is written to a file, you will need a textbox to enter text into. Click the **TextBox** control button in the **Toolbox** and draw it on the form.

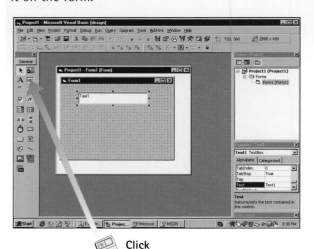

Click

3 Add a Command Button

You will also need a command button to start the output process. Click the **Command Button** control icon in the **Toolbox** and draw it on the form.

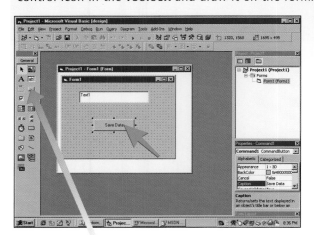

 Click

4 Print to the File

One of the methods to write data to a sequential data file is using the **Print** statement.

5 Place Data on the Same Line

When writing data to the file, you will want to have related items of data on the same line (such as first name, last name) You can do this by using the semicolon in the output statement.

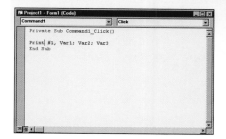

6 Using the Write Statement

The **Write** statement is another method for writing information to a file. The **Write** statement and the **Print** statement differ only in how the data is actually written to the file. Whereas the data written with the **Print** statement is space delimited, the **Write** statement data is comma delimited.

7 Write Data from a Textbox

Using the **Print** statement along with the controls you placed on the form places the data into the file. The code shown in the following figure takes any text that was entered in the textbox and writes it to the file when the command button is clicked.

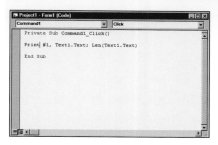

End

How-To Hints

Sequential Files

Sequential file access means that when you are accessing the file, it must be read from and written to sequentially (that is, in order—from beginning to end). This is the biggest weakness of a sequential file.

Space Delimited Versus Comma Delimited

The difference between a space-delimited and comma-delimited file is how the data is separated. A space-delimited file uses spaces to separate the text on a line. This usually causes problems if the data you are writing to the file contains spaces. A comma-delimited file uses commas to separate the data. This is usually the method that is used when writing data to a sequential file.

How to Read Data from the File

After you have data in a file, you need a way to retrieve that data. For sequential files, you should use the **Input** statement. Using this statement enables you to read the information from the file and use it in your program. The data must be read in exactly the same order and format as it was written.

Begin

1 Add a Second Textbox

To display the data from a file when it is read, you will need to add a second textbox to display. Click the **TextBox** control button in the **Toolbox** and draw it on the form.

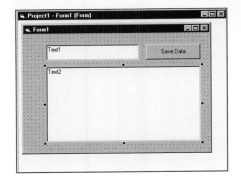

2 Set the ScrollBars Property

When you use a textbox to display data from a file, you must turn the scrollbars on for the textbox by using the **ScrollBars** property, which is set to **None** by default.

Click

3 Set the MultiLine Property

In addition to turning on scrollbars, you must set the textbox to display the data on multiple lines. You can do this by setting the **MultiLine** property to **True**.

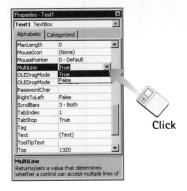

Click

4 Open the File for Input

To read the data from the file, you must first open it for input by using the **For Input** option of the **Open** statement.

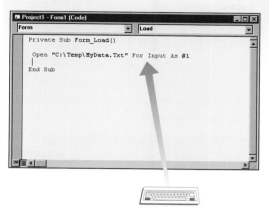

5 Read the Data

Reading data from the file is as simple as using the **Input** statement.

6 Place the Data in the Textbox

During the process of reading the data into the program, you will want to add the code that moves the data into the textbox. In addition, you will be using the **vbCrLf** constant to place the data on separate lines.

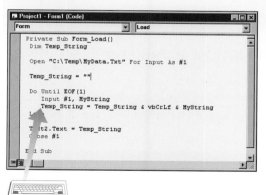

End

How-To Hints

Reading Data into Variables

If you want to read data correctly from a file into variables, use the **Write** statement instead of the **Print** statement when writing the data into the file.

How to Use Random Files

Opening a file for random access enables you to read from or write to the file at any point in the file. This provides you with control over how you access the data in the file. This differs from a sequential file, which must be read from the beginning to the end whenever you need to get data from it.

Begin

1 Open the Random File

Opening a random file is a little different than opening a sequential file. Using the **For Random** option requires other options that will be covered in the next few steps.

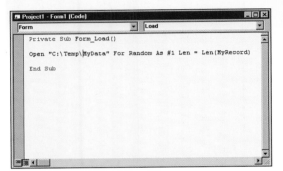

2 Create a User–Defined Type

Because random files can read and write a record of information, user-defined types are used to group all the related variables together into one record.

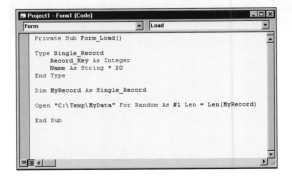

3 Set the Len Parameter

The **Len** parameter is required by the **Open** statement when using random files to specify the total number of characters included in one record.

4 Using the Put Statement

To write data to a random file, use the **Put** statement instead of the **Print** or **Write** statements. The **Put** statement requires the record number that the data will be written to.

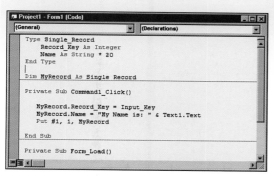

```
Type Single_Record
    Record_Key As Integer
    Name As String * 20
End Type

Dim MyRecord As Single Record

Private Sub Command1_Click()

    MyRecord.Record_Key = Input_Key
    MyRecord.Name = "My Name is: " & Text1.Text
    Put #1, 1, MyRecord

End Sub

Private Sub Form_Load()
```

5 Using the Get Statement

To read data from the random file, use the **Get** statement instead of the **Input** statement. In addition, specify the record number to read.

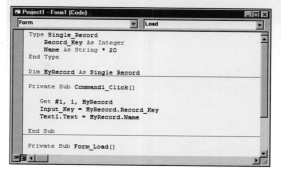

```
Type Single_Record
    Record_Key As Integer
    Name As String * 20
End Type

Dim MyRecord As Single Record

Private Sub Command1_Click()

    Get #1, 1, MyRecord
    Input_Key = MyRecord.Record_Key
    Text1.Text = MyRecord.Name

End Sub

Private Sub Form_Load()
```

End

How-To Hints

Random Access Files

The closest you can come to a database without actually using one is to use random access files in your application. The only thing to remember is that you control everything that happens to that file.

User-Defined Types

A user-defined type is actually a collection of variables grouped together under a single variable name. This enables you to read and write the group as a single variable. The following example can be read from and written to a random access file:

```
Public Type SystemInfo
    CPU As Variant
    Memory As Long
    VideoColors As Integer
    Cost As Currency
    PurchaseDate As Variant
End Type
```

Project

This project shows you how to create a simple phone book application that you can use. It will hold the following information:

✓ Name

✓ Address

As you follow the steps in this project, you will start a new Visual Basic project; design an input form; and add the code needed to open, read, write, and close the file that you are using to hold the information.

After you have created the form and typed in all the code shown, you will have a functional address book that you can use to store information to a data file on your hard drive. This project demonstrates the use of conditional logic, array processing, input and output, variables, controls, and finally file I/O, bringing together everything that you have learned in this book.

1 Start a New Project

To start a new project, start Visual Basic, choose **New** from the **File** menu, select **Standard EXE** from the **New Project** dialog, and click **OK**.

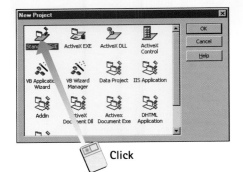

Click

2 Add the Textboxes

To display information and enter new information into the application, you need to add six textboxes to the default form as shown the following figure.

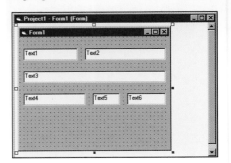

3 Set the Textbox Properties

After you have added the textboxes to the form, change the **Name** property of each textbox as listed.

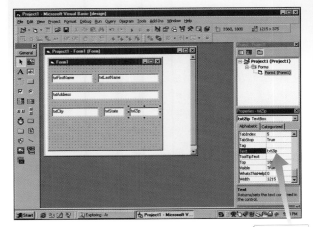

4 Add the Labels

To know what each textbox is displaying, place six labels on the form, one above each textbox.

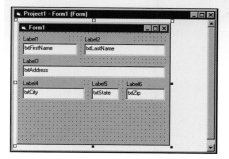

5 Set the Label Captions

For each of the six labels you have added, set the **Caption** property as listed.

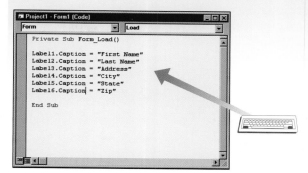

```
Private Sub Form_Load()

Label1.Caption = "First Name"
Label2.Caption = "Last Name"
Label3.Caption = "Address"
Label4.Caption = "City"
Label5.Caption = "State"
Label6.Caption = "Zip"

End Sub
```

6 Add the Command Buttons

The final group of controls to add to the form is the command buttons. There are four of them and should be added as shown in the following figure.

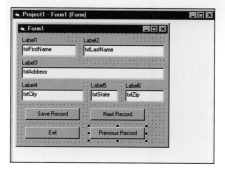

7 Set the Command Button

There are two properties you must set for each command button: **Name** and **Caption**. Set the **Caption** properties as shown on the command buttons in the previous step. Using the **Properties window**, set the **Name** property for each command button as listed in Notepad in the following figure.

```
Command1 : cmdSaveRec
Command2 : cmdNextRec
Command3 : cmdExit
Command4 : cmdPrevRec
```

Continues

8 Define the Variables

Several variables must be defined to enable the application to execute properly. These are used to hold the record number being processed, the length of the record, and the channel number used to reference the file.

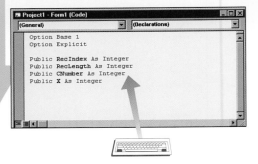

9 Add a Code Module

The definition for a constant or a custom data type must be placed in a code module. To add a code module, right-click the **Project Explorer** and choose **Add** from the pop-up menu. The **Add Module** dialog appears. Select **Module** from the **New** tab.

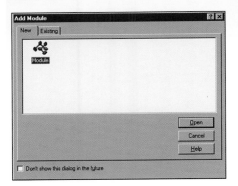

10 Define a Public Constant

Use the **MaxRecords** constant to specify the maximum number of records the data file will be able to hold.

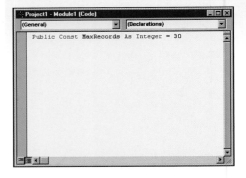

11 Set the Record Type

In addition, you must define a custom data type that will contain the data for each entry in the data file.

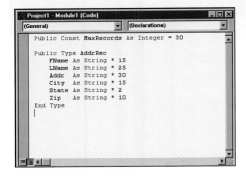

12 Define the Record Array

After you have defined the new record type, you can use it to define the array that will be used to contain the data read from the file.

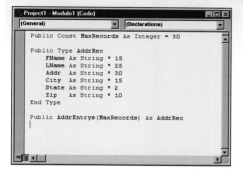

```
Public Const MaxRecords As Integer = 30

Public Type AddrRec
    FName As String * 15
    LName As String * 25
    Addr  As String * 30
    City  As String * 15
    State As String * 2
    Zip   As String * 10
End Type

Public AddrEntrys(MaxRecords) As AddrRec
```

13 Add the Save Record Event

When you type information into the form's textboxes, it must be saved or written to the data file. This event will open the data file for random access, write the record to the file, and then close the file.

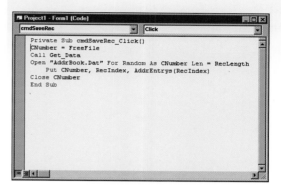

```
Private Sub cmdSaveRec_Click()
CNumber = FreeFile
Call Get_Data
Open "AddrBook.Dat" For Random As CNumber Len = RecLength
    Put CNumber, RecIndex, AddrEntrys(RecIndex)
Close CNumber
End Sub
```

14 Add the Update_Form Procedure

Whenever you move from one record to another in the data array, you must move the information from the array to the textboxes on the form. This procedure will move the data to the form and is called from the next and previous event routines.

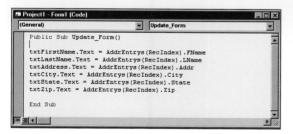

```
Public Sub Update_Form()

txtFirstName.Text = AddrEntrys(RecIndex).FName
txtLastName.Text = AddrEntrys(RecIndex).LName
txtAddress.Text = AddrEntrys(RecIndex).Addr
txtCity.Text = AddrEntrys(RecIndex).City
txtState.Text = AddrEntrys(RecIndex).State
txtZip.Text = AddrEntrys(RecIndex).Zip

End Sub
```

15 Add to the Form_Load Event

In order to view the data already in the data file, you must load the data into the array. This is accomplished by using a **For** loop statement group. This routine also checks to see whether the file is empty and initializes the array accordingly. At the same time, you will be initializing a few variables to start the process.

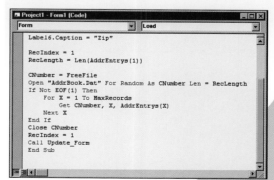

```
Label16.Caption = "Zip"

RecIndex = 1
RecLength = Len(AddrEntrys(1))

CNumber = FreeFile
Open "AddrBook.Dat" For Random As CNumber Len = RecLength
If Not EOF(1) Then
    For X = 1 To MaxRecords
        Get CNumber, X, AddrEntrys(X)
    Next X
End If
Close CNumber
RecIndex = 1
Call Update_Form
End Sub
```

Continues

Project Continued

16 Add the Get_Data Procedure

Whenever you move from one record to another, you want to be able to save any changes made to the previous record before you move to the new one. This procedure is called from the next and previous event routines.

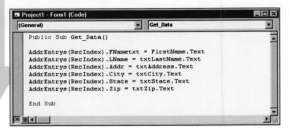

```
Project1 - Form1 (Code)
(General)                        Get_Data

    Public Sub Get_Data()

    AddrEntrys(RecIndex).FNametxt = FirstName.Text
    AddrEntrys(RecIndex).LName = txtLastName.Text
    AddrEntrys(RecIndex).Addr = txtAddress.Text
    AddrEntrys(RecIndex).City = txtCity.Text
    AddrEntrys(RecIndex).State = txtState.Text
    AddrEntrys(RecIndex).Zip = txtZip.Text

    End Sub
```

17 Add the Next Record Event

Before moving to the next record, check to see whether you are already displaying the last record. If you can move forward to a new record, save the data currently displayed using the **Get_Data** routine; then the **Update_Form** routine is called to display the new record on the form.

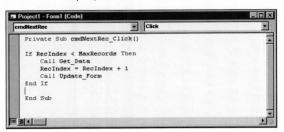

```
Project1 - Form1 (Code)
cmdNextRec                       Click

    Private Sub cmdNextRec_Click()

    If RecIndex < MaxRecords Then
        Call Get_Data
        RecIndex = RecIndex + 1
        Call Update_Form
    End If

    End Sub
```

18 Add the Previous Record Event

Before moving to the previous record, check to see whether you are at the beginning of the file. If you can move backward to a new record, save the data currently displayed using the **Get_Data** routine; then the **Update_Form** routine is called to display the new record on the form.

```
Project1 - Form1 (Code)
cmdPrevRec                       Click

    Private Sub cmdPrevRec_Click()

    If RecIndex > 1 Then
        Call Get_Data
        RecIndex = RecIndex - 1
        Call Update_Form
    End If

    End Sub
```

19 Add the Quit Event

When you exit the program, all the data in the array should be written back into the file to save any changes made.

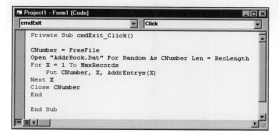

```
Private Sub cmdExit_Click()

CNumber = FreeFile
Open "AddrBook.Dat" For Random As CNumber Len = RecLength
For X = 1 To MaxRecords
    Put CNumber, X, AddrEntrys(X)
Next X
Close CNumber
End

End Sub
```

20 Run the Application

Finally, run the application, add an entry to the form, and click the **Save** command button. Then quit the application and restart it to see that the data you entered was saved and redisplayed.

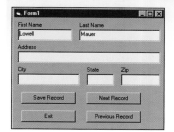

End

Task

19

Accessing Database Information

Visual Basic enables you to create database maintenance screens quickly and easily. In fact, Visual Basic includes a wizard that will generate screens for you. The idea is that you identify where your database resides and the fields you want on your form. Visual Basic has the capability of reading your database definition as well as the data. Visual Basic will allow you to read two types of databases. The first type is known as a Jet database engine—this is the database interface that is native to Visual Basic. Microsoft Access utilizes the same Jet engine, so creating a link becomes very easy.

The other type of database is one that supports Open Database Connectivity (ODBC). Visual Basic utilizes ODBC to create a link to the database and have access to the files, fields, and relationships. This section reviews the use of data controls and database access and covers the Biblio.MDB Access database, which is a sample database that comes with Visual Basic. ●

How to Use the Data Control

The Data control provides your application with a link to your file definition. When you select the Data control, you must identify where your database is located and what information you want to access. The Data control will also provide your application with the ability to navigate through your database records.

1 Using the DatabaseName Property

The **DatabaseName** property contains the fully qualified name of your database. To be fully qualified requires that you identify the full pathname where your database resides. Using the **ellipsis** button in the property will present a dialog box for you to choose your database.

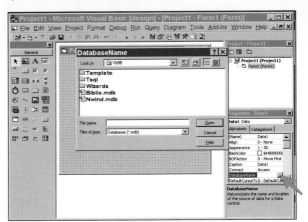

2 Using the RecordSource Property

RecordSource identifies to your application which table you are selecting from your database. If you require that data fields from multiple tables be selected, **RecordSource** supports Structured Query Language (SQL). You can enter SQL statements to extract your fields.

3 Navigate Through Your Records

The Data control object uses four buttons, which allow you to maneuver through your records. These buttons are designed similarly to a VCR or CD player. You can move forward or backward slowly or quickly.

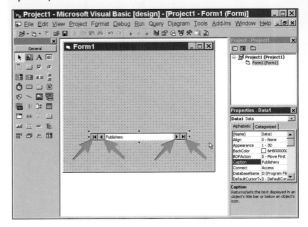

4 Using BOF/EOF Actions

BOF (Beginning of File) and EOF (End of File) actions are the options that exist when your data reaches the first or last transaction of your file.

5 Using the RecordsetType Property

The **RecordsetType** property identifies the type of file that Visual Basic will work with. **0 – Table** includes all the records in your database table. **1 – Dynaset** is an extract from one or more files from your database. Finally, **2 – Snapshot** provides a read-only copy of data that is stored in memory.

6 Using the Connect Property

The **Connect** property identifies the type of database that you are connecting to.

End

How-To Hints

Search vs. Set

Setting the database name to the fully qualified name in the **DatabaseName** property will cause Visual Basic to search for the database in that path. During runtime, it's best to allow the user to select the path of the database and set it programmatically.

Dynasets

When you use a dynaset file, you must provide SQL or Querydef to define your data. This method allows you to use fields from multiple files. However, any changes made will not be reflected until a refresh is complete.

Tables

Using tables has the advantage of immediate update; this is particularly advantageous in a multiuser environment. However, you must select the entire table, and you cannot include fields from other files.

Snapshots

Snapshots represent a copy of your selected data brought into memory. Since it resides in memory, it will be much faster to locate records. However, you cannot update these records.

How to Use Bound Controls

Now that you have reviewed the Data control and identified your database to Visual Basic and Data controls such as TextBox and Label, it's time to combine these controls and generate data screens. You will learn how to assign a database field to a control on your form. This action, which is called binding, uses controls that have binding properties. As an example, a textbox bound to a database field displays the value of that field for the current record. As you move through your database using the navigation controls, the value of the textbox will change to the value of the current record. This section will review the bound controls and how to create forms.

Begin

1 Using the Textbox Control

The TextBox is an updatable control. Because this control allows users to type or do data entry, it is ideal for displaying information that a user can change.

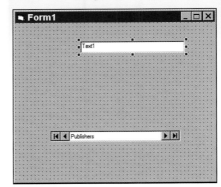

2 Using the Label Control

The Label control allows you to bind fields that are viewable only. Remember that the user does not have the capability to type in a label field. This can be used for information that the user should not have access to change—such as a Social Security number in a personnel file.

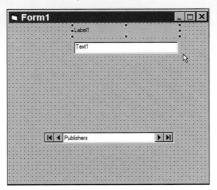

3 Using the DataSource Property

The **DataSource** property contains the name of the Data control object. This instructs the control where to search for the data fields. The drop-down box displays the names of your Data controls.

4 Using the DataField Property

The **DataField** property contains the data field that you want displayed in the control. The drop-down box enables you to select from a list of valid fields from the data source.

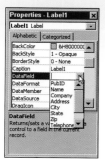

5 Delete Data

The **Delete** method allows you to remove transactions from your database. After you remove a record from your database, you use the **MoveNext** or **MoveLast** methods to move to your next or previous record of your database.

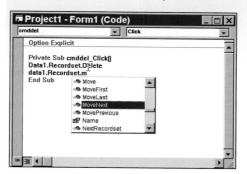

6 Add New Records

When you need to add new records, you want to bring up a blank screen for data entry. The **AddNew** method creates a blank screen where you can enter new transactions.

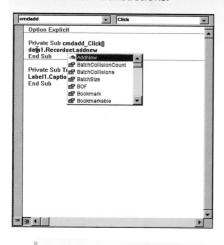

7 Update Existing Records

When you type over an existing data field of a record and move to a new record or close the form, your data will automatically be updated.

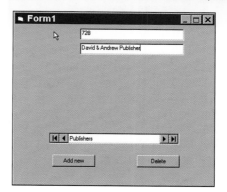

End

How-To Hints

Identify Yourself

In order to use the **DataField** property, you must enter a data source. The data field works in conjunction with the data source. It allows Visual Basic to identify which data fields are available.

How to Use Data Grids

The DataGrid is a control that allows you to view data in rows and columns. This control creates a spreadsheet display allowing users to update individual cells. Visual Basic 6 has introduced a new data method called ADO (ActiveX Data Objects). ADO provides a new way of generating grid screens and forms. The ADO data access method requires an additional step—you need to define the ODBC (Open Database Connectivity) driver to Visual Basic. This section reviews how to set up ADO controls and ODBC data access.

Begin

1 Set Up ODBC

Your **Control Panel** has the ODBC setup. Select **Control Panel** from the **Setting** options of the **Start** menu. Select the **ODBC (32bit)** icon.

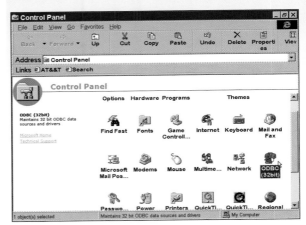

2 Add BIBLIO DSN

From the **ODBC Data Source Adminstrator** screen, select the **New** option. This will allow you to create a new data source (and brings you to the **Create New Data Source** dialog box).

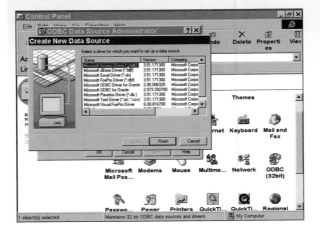

3 Select the Microsoft Access Driver

The BIBLIO database is an Access database; you are assigning the rules of Access to a name that will be used by Visual Basic. It is a file definition that associates ODBC to the database.

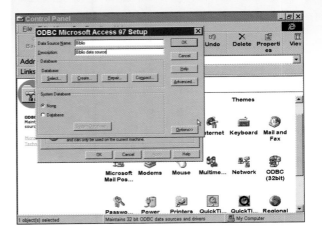

4 Using the ADO Data Control

The ADO Data Control looks similar to the Data control you have seen before. However, it provides you with additional capabilities, and requires the ODBC data access driver. The ADO controls are not available in the standard control set. To add them to your **Toolbox**, select **Components** from the **Project** menu. Check the box for **Microsoft ADO Data Control 6.0 (OLEDB)**. This will add this control to your **Toolbox**.

5 Define the ADO Data Source

When you add the new ADO Data Control to your form, you will notice that the properties are not the same as the Data control initially discussed. To define the source and some additional capability, right-click the ADO Data Control and select **ADODC Properties**.

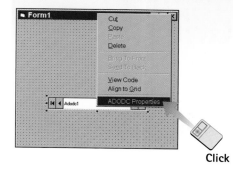

Click

6 Click the General Tab

Under the **General** tab you define the ODBC driver that you defined. The **ODBC Data Source Name** you choose is the name you created when you set up ODBC. This instructs Visual Basic which file should be used.

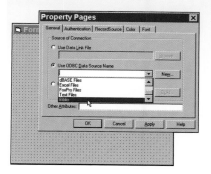

7 Click the RecordSource Tab

The **RecordSource** tab allows you to select the data source to be associated to the Record control.

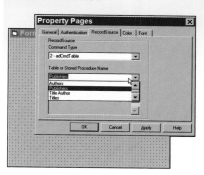

End

How to Use Data Grids, Part II

So far, you have only learned how to prepare for the Data control used for a data grid. The ADO Data Control can be used to create the online screens that were discussed in the previous sections; however, it also provides the additional capability of generating data grids. This section reviews how to produce and work with a data grid.

Begin

1 Add the DataGrid Control

The DataGrid control is also an added control not included with your basic **Toolbox**. To add it, right-click on an empty area of your **Toolbox**, and select **Components**. Check the **Microsoft DataGrid Control 6.0 (OLEDB)** and click **OK**.

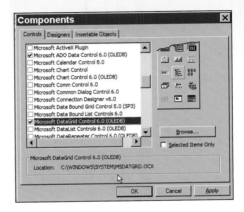

2 Using the DataSource Property

The DataGrid control is added the same way that all the other controls are added. Enter the ADO name in the **DataSource** property. If you review the properties, you will notice that it does not include a data field property. That's because the grid can display multiple fields.

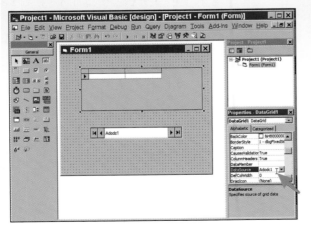

3 Retrieve Fields

When you right-click the data grid, there is an option to **Retrieve Fields** from the menu. This will automatically populate your spreadsheet.

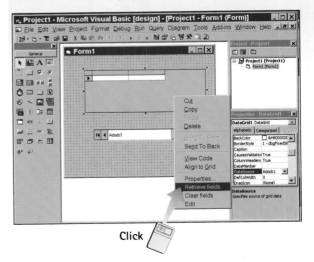

Click

4 Access the DataGrid Control

To access the properties for the DataGrid control, right-click the grid and select **Properties** from the pop-up menu. You will notice that some of the properties are also available in the **Properties window**; however, choosing from the pop-up menu provides additional property options.

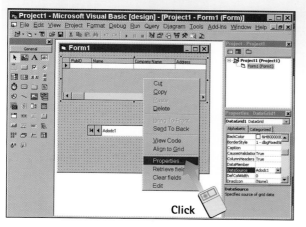

Click

5 Click the General Tab

The **General** tab of the **Property Pages** dialog allows you to control the look and feel of your spreadsheet. From the title to the editability of the spreadsheet itself, you select the options.

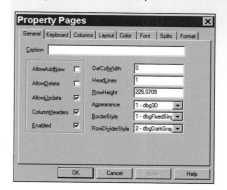

6 Click the Columns Tab

The **Columns** tab allows you to design the column order and column headings of the spreadsheet.

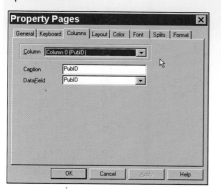

7 Column Edit

When you right-click the data grid, you can change the mode of the menu to edit—after selecting **Edit**, the menu will disappear. However, when you right-click the grid again, you have the option of adding or deleting columns from your spreadsheet.

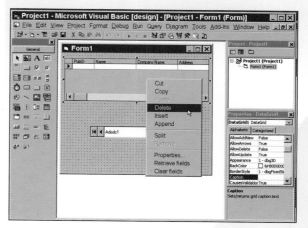

End

How to Use the Data Report

With what you have accomplished to this point, you can display data to a screen for viewing or updating. Most, if not all, applications need to be able to generate reports that can be printed and distributed. Visual Basic has a data reporting capability called a data report. As with forms and grids, you need to define and associate the data source with the data report. This section reviews how to define your data source and associate them to your data report.

Begin

1 Select a Recordset

The recordset for a data report is similar in concept to the dynaset that was used in the Data control. It contains data fields that are presented in your report. Recordsets are created using SQL. Using a query tool to select your records gives you the flexibility of limiting your recordset selection.

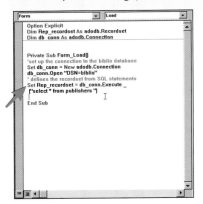

2 Connect to the Database

In order to generate reports, you must first define the ODBC driver that defines the data source. After your connection is made and the database is opened, SQL will populate the recordset.

3 Add Data to the Report

After your recordset has been created, you can add fields from the recordset to your data report. The data report acts similar to a form. In fact, you add a data report from the **Project** menu the same way you add a form—just click **Add Data Report**.

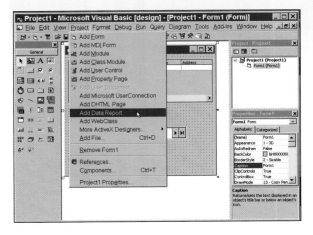

4 Using the Data Report Layout

The data report is set up with several pre-defined sections:

Report Header—Displays information once at the top of the report.

Page Header—Is information that will be displayed on the top of each page of your report.

Detail Section—Also known as the report body, contains your detail report information.

Page Footer—Displays information at the bottom of each page of your report.

Report Footer—Displays information at the bottom of your report only on the last page.

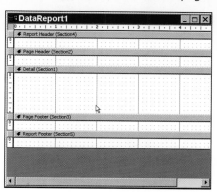

5 Using the Data Report Controls

Just as you used controls to design and paint your forms, you also used report controls to define each section of your report. The data report is generated based on the controls that are added. You paint your report output the same way you paint your screens.

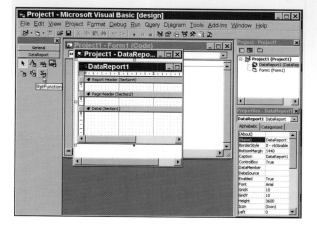

6 Populate the Reports

After you have designed your report and placed the controls where you want them, you want the data from your recordset to populate the controls. The **Show** method will display the populated report.

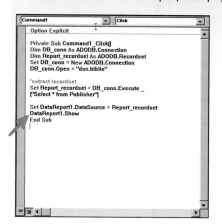

How-To Hints

Limiting Data Retrieval

With SQL, you can limit the transactions that are retrieved from your database using the **Where** clause. You can also select information from multiple related datasets.

End

How to Use the Data Report, Part II

The data report comes with its own set of **Toolbox** controls. These controls are similar to the controls that are used to generate forms. The controls can be used in your report to instruct Visual Basic where to display your information. The data report also includes several predefined mathematical functions and data elements that are available for you to use in the controls.

Begin

1 Using the RptTextBox Control

The RptTextBox control is used to display information fields from your recordset. You need to bind or assign a data element from your recordset to the RptTextBox object. In the **DataField** property in the **Properties window**, enter the fieldname of the element you want displayed.

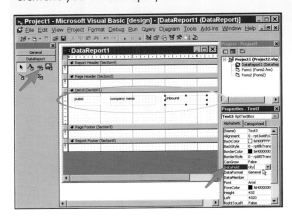

2 Using the RptLabel Control

The RptLabel control is used to display information that is not associated or bound to your database information. It is used for report headings and footings, as well as column headings. You also use RptLabel to display predefined data elements such as date and time, in addition to built-in functions such as counts and totals.

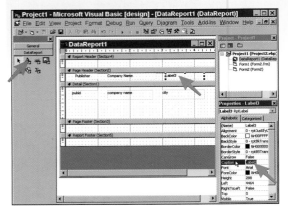

3 Using the RptImage Control

The RptImage control displays pictures on your report. After you add the control to your report, use the **ellipsis** button on the **Picture** property. This will display the **Load Picture** dialog box where you can select the image you want displayed.

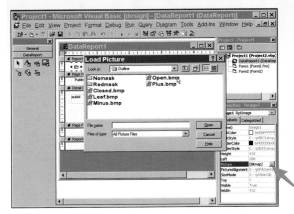

4 Using RptShape and RptLine Controls

The RptShape and RptLine controls are similar to their form counterparts Shape and Line. They can be used for underlining data or headings, and displaying a variety of shapes to your report.

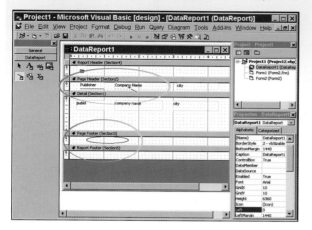

5 Using the RptFunction Control

The RptFunction control has several predefined functions that can be used in your report. The **DataField** property contains the field name that the function will be performed on. The **FunctionType** property selects which function to perform.

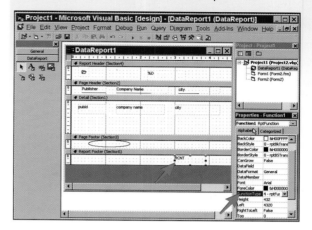

6 Using the System Data Elements

The data report provides several system information items stored in available data elements. These elements can be incorporated into your label controls:

%d—Current date as 1/1/99
%D—Current date as Friday, January 1, 1999
%t—Current time as 14:15:00
%T—Current time as 2:15:00 PM
%p—Current page number
%P—Total number of pages
%I—The report title (this is the **Title** property for the **Data Report** object).

How-To Hints

RptTextBox

When you add the RptTextBox control to your detail section, you only need to draw that control once. Visual Basic will generate a column, and the data element value will be displayed for the record in your database.

Functions

The current available functions can only be utilized in the **Report Footer** section. The function will create its value after having processed all the data in the source.

End

Project

In this project, you will review the database access. You will use the Biblio database file and create input screens, as well as a data grid. You will generate input and update and delete capabilities for the file. You will generate the maintenance forms and see them in action.

1 Start a New Project

Select the **Standard EXE** option from the Visual Basic **New Project** screen. Name the form **frmmain** and give it the caption **Biblio Maintenance Screen**. Increase the size of the screen.

2 Add the Data Control

Let's add the Data control to the data form. **Name** the Data control **dat_titles**, and change the **Caption** to **book titles**.

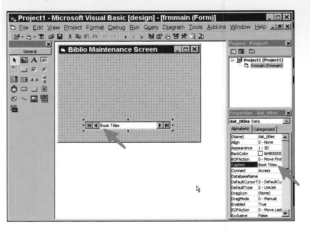

3 Make the Data Connection

Now you need to associate the Data control to the database name. Select the **DatabaseName** property and click the **ellipsis**.

Click

4 Select the Biblio Database

Select the Biblio.MDB file; it should be in your Visual Basic library. You can use the **Find** command if you are having trouble locating the file. Click the **Open** button and notice that the fully qualified name now appears in the **DatabaseName** property.

5 Choose the Data Source

Now that you have connected the database name, select the data source—that is, the Data control connection to the textbox—through the **DataSource** property.

6 Record Source

So as of now, the Data control is assigned to a database. The TextBox control is assigned to the Data control. The textbox will know which files are associated to the Data control. Select **Titles** in the **RecordSource** property.

7 Select the BOF/EOF Actions

Review the **BOFAction** (beginning of file action) and **EOFAction** (end of file action) properties.

Continues

8 Draw a Textbox

Draw a textbox on the form and assign the data field; the data is known from the record source that you just assigned.

Select the **Title** field.

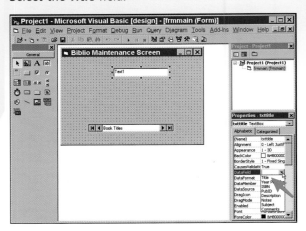

9 Choose a Data Field

Let's add another textbox and assign it the **Description DataField**.

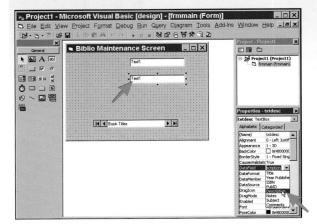

10 Create More Data Fields

Go ahead and create three more textboxes and assign the following data fields to them: **Title**, **ISBN**, **PubID**. After you have created these fields, select them all. You will see that they are all highlighted.

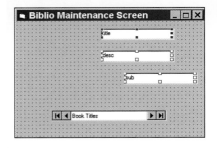

11 Align the Properties

From the **Format** menu, select **Align** and then **Rights**. This will align your properties. If you want, you can also drag one box with your mouse, which will move all your selected items.

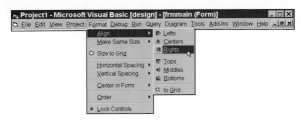

12 Create Labels and Add Buttons

Now create three Label controls, placing one next to each of the text boxes as descriptive fields for the textboxes. When you're done, align these controls as well.

Now add two command buttons. You can call the first one **cmdadd** with a caption of **Add Record** (entered in the **Caption** property in the **Properties window**). Call the other button **cmddel**, with the **Caption** of **Delete Record**.

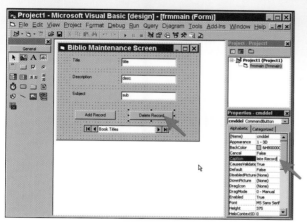

13 Add Command Buttons

At this point, you need to save the project. Run your application—you can see that you can retrieve and update data already.

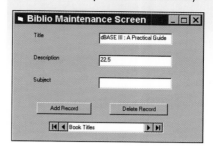

14 Notice the Update Data

Select any transaction, change a field, move to the next record, and then move back. You will see that the change has been done. You could even exit your application, restart it, and notice the updated record.

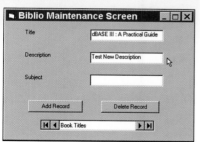

15 Add Some Code

You did all of that without even adding a letter of code. Now add the following code for the CMDADD and CMDDEL buttons.

```
cmddel                              Click

Option Explicit

Private Sub cmdadd_Click()
'set up a blank record to add to database
dat_titles.Recordset.AddNew
End Sub

Private Sub cmddel_Click()
dat_titles.Recordset.Delete
'display next record
dat_titles.Recordset.MoveNext

End Sub
```

Continues

16 Add Records

Run your application again and notice that the **Add Record** button actually brings up a blank screen for your data entry. Now, try to delete a record. You have just completed a maintenance screen. You can now select any database with any files and generate an application.

17 Open the Control Panel

Now you want to use the advanced ActiveX Data Object for a data grid. You will be setting up an ODBC connection. From your **Start** menu, select **Settings** and then **Control Panel**.

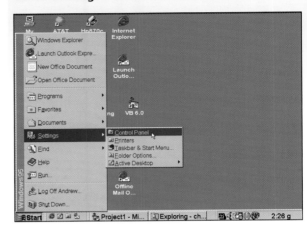

18 Select ODBC

Now click the **ODBC 32bit** icon—you can think of this as defining your database connection.

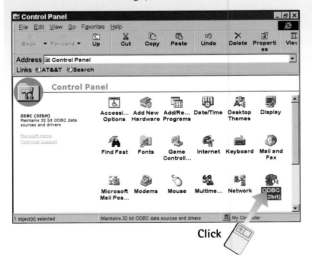

Click

19 Assign the Data Source for ODBC

Choose the **Microsoft Access Driver** in the **User Data Sources** area, and then assign the Biblio database to it. Click **Configure**. The data source name will be utilized in Visual Basic. That will let Visual Basic know which driver to use and where the database source is.

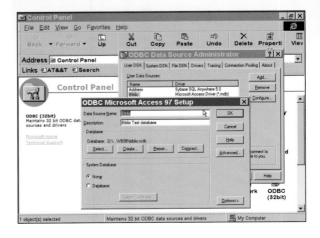

20 Add the ADO Data Control

Right-click any empty space in your **Toolbox** and select **Components** from the pop-up menu. Add the **Microsoft ADO Data Control 6.0 (OLEDB)** from the **Components** dialog box by clicking its checkbox.

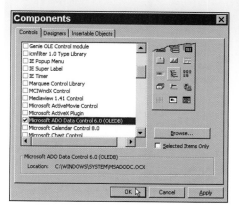

21 Select the Data Grid Control

While you have the **Controls** tab of the **Components** dialog box open, also select the **Microsoft DataGrid Control 6.0 (OLEDB)**. Then click **OK**. Also remember to do a save.

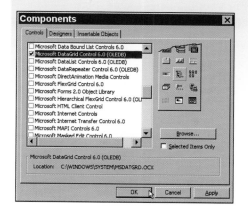

22 Add a New Form

Let's now add a new form. From the **Project** menu, select **Add Form**.

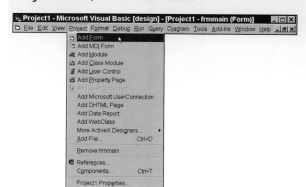

23 Select the Data Source

Right-click the ADO Data Control and select the **Properties** option. Under the **General** tab of the **Propery Pages**, select the Biblio ODBC driver as your data source.

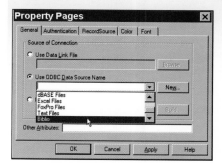

Continues

24 Click the RecordSource Tab

Go to the **RecordSource** tab and select a
Table or Stored Procedure Name and the
Command Type of option **2 – adCmdTable**. You are
choosing a database table.

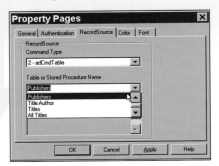

25 Add a Data Grid

Click the **DataGrid** control button to select
a data grid and add it to your form.

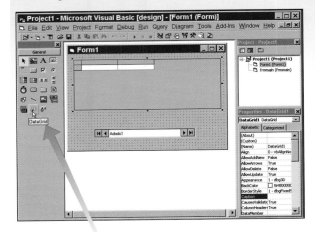

Click

26 Choose the Data Source for ADO

Using the **DataSource** property's drop-
down box in the **Properties window**, select the name
of the ADO control.

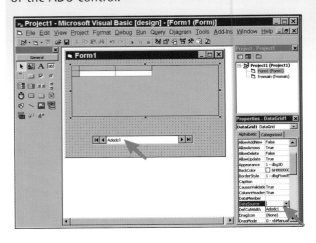

27 Get Data

Right-click anywhere on the data grid.
Select the **Retrieve Fields** option.

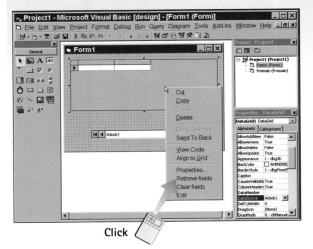

Click

28 Populate Headings

Visual Basic will display a message box asking if you want to replace your layout—click **Yes**. You will notice that the column headings are the field names of your data source.

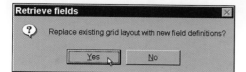

29 Populate Data

Run your application and you will see that the grid is populated with data. You can set the properties in the ADO Data Control to add, update, or delete from the grid.

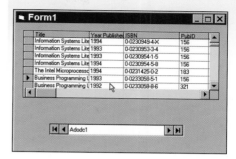

End

Task

CHAPTER 20

Using Visual Basic Add-Ins

*L*ike many other Windows application development tools, Visual Basic contains many features, functions, and wizards that help make it easier for you to design, create, test, and deliver a professional Windows application. Many of these programs and wizards, as well as standalone programs, are accessible from within Visual Basic. Many of these are added to the Visual Basic environment by using the **Add-In Manager** to select and load the selected functions.

The **Add-In Manager** lists all of the available add-ins that are installed on your computer. What you will see in this chapter is how to use some of the more useful add-ins that come with Visual Basic itself. ●

How to Use the Add-In Manager

The **Add-In Manager** is the tool that you will use to register an add-in, load or unload it, and set its load behavior. By doing this, you will then be able to access the add-in from within Visual Basic.

Begin

1 Start the Add-In Manager

To open the **Add-In Manager**, pull down the **Add-Ins** menu and choose **Add-In Manager**.

Click

2 View Available Add-Ins

All of the available wizards and add-ins are listed in the **Add-In Manager** dialog for you to choose from.

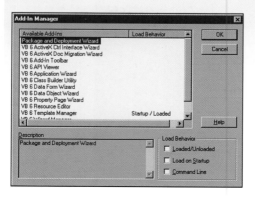

3 Load an Add-In

To make an add-in available, select it and click the **Loaded/Unloaded** checkbox.

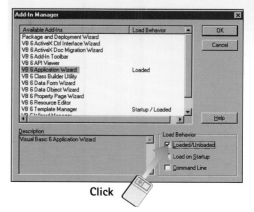

Click

4 Load an Add-In at Startup

An add-in can also be made available automatically when Visual Basic starts by selecting the **Load on Startup** checkbox.

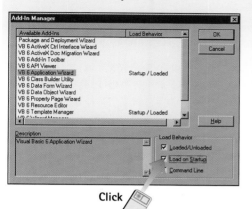

Click

5 Finish the Process

After specifying the add-ins you want, click **OK** to have them added to the **Add-Ins** menu in Visual Basic.

End

How-To Hints

Command Line Add-Ins

There are times that you will be executing Visual Basic from a command line or script when running very long tests on an application. The **Command Line** option to load an add-in allows you to have it loaded only when the Visual Basic environment was started from a command line or script.

How to Use the Application Wizard

The Application Wizard is one of the most powerful wizards that you can use in Visual Basic. By using the Application Wizard, you can create a functioning application shell that includes all of the common elements of any Windows application that you might need for a complete Windows application. The only things you need to add are the actual program code and forms that are unique to your application.

Begin

1 Start the Application Wizard

To use the Application Wizard, pull down the **File** menu and choose **New Project** to display the **New Project** dialog. Then select the **VB Application Wizard** and click **OK**. When the **Introduction** dialog is displayed, click **Next** to continue.

2 Select the Interface

You can now select the interface to use for your application. A short description and image is displayed when you select each of the different types. In addition, you can name the project you are creating. Select the **Multiple Document Interface (MDI)** checkbox and enter an application name. Then click **Next**.

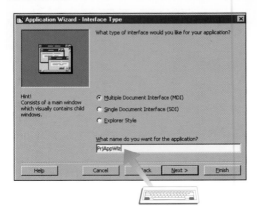

3 Add the Menu Items

The **Menus** options allow you to select the main menu items and their respective **Sub Menus** for your application. Also, if you need an item that is not listed, you can add it. Using the defaults, click **Next** to continue.

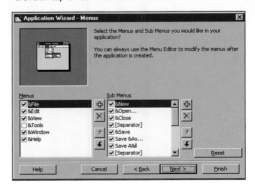

4 Include a Toolbar

Adding a toolbar to the application is as simple as selecting the buttons you want on it. Leaving the default selections, click the **Next** button three times. This will bypass two dialogs, accepting their default values.

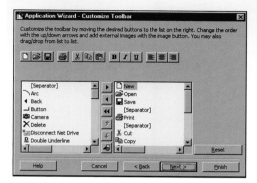

5 Choose Forms

The **Standard Forms** dialog allows you to add other forms you need to the application, such as the **Splash Screen** and **About Box** forms. Select these two forms and click **Next**.

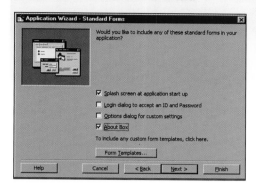

6 Access a Database

Clicking the **Create New Form** button will start the Data Form Wizard, which helps you create forms that access information from a database. Click the **Finish** button to actually create the application.

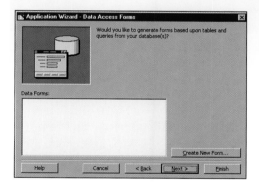

7 Work with the New Application

You now have the beginning of a complete application. All you need to do is add the required code.

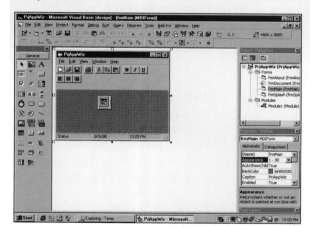

End

How to Use the Data Form Wizard

The Data Form Wizard helps you create forms that include all the necessary code and controls to access information from a database file or system. When a form is created, you can actually run the program and add, modify, or delete information from the database without writing any code yourself. The Data Form Wizard can be started from one of three places. You have already seen that it can be accessed from the Application Wizard. It can also be started by choosing it from the **Add-Ins** menu; or you can right-click the **Project Explorer** window, select **Add**, and then choose **Form** to display the **Add Form** dialog. You would then select the **VB Data Form Wizard** and click **OK**.

Begin

1 Start the Data Form Wizard

In an existing application, choose **Data Form Wizard** from the **Add-Ins** menu. Then click **Next** to bypass the **Introduction** dialog.

Click

2 Choose the Database Type

Select the type of database access you will be using. For this task, choose **Access** and click **Next**.

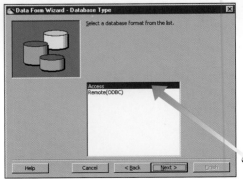

Click

3 Specify the File or Connection

The next step is to select the database to use. For this task, locate the **NWIND.MDB** database file using the **Browse** button, and then select it. Click **Next** to continue.

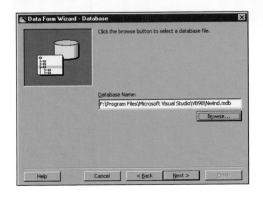

4 Name the Data Form

Enter the name you want the form to be called. Then, using the defaults for the other options, click **Next** to continue.

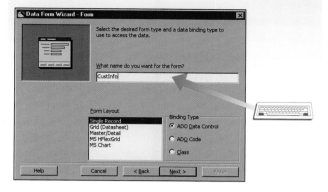

5 Select the Record Source

From the **Record Source** drop-down listbox, select the **Customers** table. Then choose the fields you want to display and how you want them sorted. When you are satisfied with your choices, click **Next**.

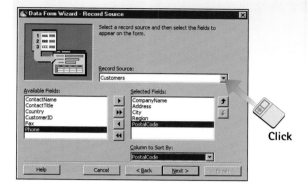

Click

6 Add the Action Buttons

Depending on the form you are creating, you can have one or more command buttons displayed. Select the buttons you want on the form and click **Finish** to create the new form.

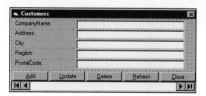

7 Work with the New Form

The new form is created with all the necessary code to display and modify the data from the database.

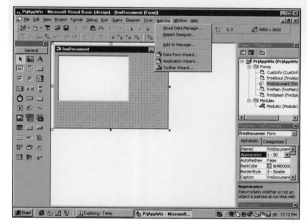

End

How-To Hints

ADO Data Control or Code?

The ADO Data Control provides the functions and buttons to allow you to move from record to record within the data without having any code in the application itself. If you choose not to use the ADO Data Control, the **ADO Code** option will add controls to the form that will duplicate the functionality of the ADO Data Control without actually using it.

How to Use the Toolbar Wizard

The Toolbar Wizard adds toolbars to a form in a project the same way the Application Wizard does. In fact, the Toolbar Wizard is only available on the **Add-Ins** menu when the Application Wizard has been loaded. The Toolbar Wizard adds the ToolBar control and the code required to recognize which button the user clicked.

Begin

1 Start the Toolbar Wizard

To add a toolbar to a form, pull down the **Add-Ins** menu and choose the **Toolbar Wizard**. The **Introduction** dialog will be displayed. Click **Next** to bypass it.

Click

2 Select the Button Images

Select the images that you want to add to the toolbar and then click the right arrow to move them to the toolbar.

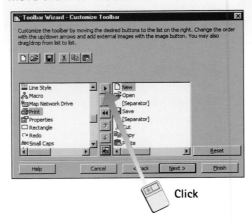

Click

3 Add a New Image

If you want to use an image that is not displayed, click the **External Image** button to select the image file you want. The **Open Image File** dialog appears. Choose the image you want and then click **Open**. Then click **Finish** to complete the creation process.

Click

4 Access the Toolbar Code

The toolbar is added to the active form along with the **ButtonClick** code needed to respond when the user clicks a button. All you need to do is add the code to perform the required actions.

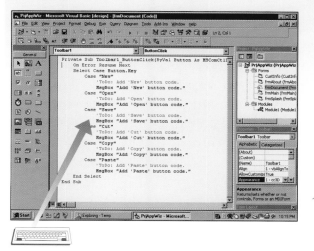

5 Display the Property Pages

A button menu is a group of options that is displayed as a drop-down list whenever the user clicks a single button on the **Toolbar**. To add a button menu, right-click the **Toolbar** to display the **Property Pages**. Then click the **Buttons** tab to display the button properties.

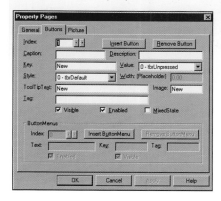

6 Add a Button Menu

A button menu is created by setting the button **Style** property to **tbrDropdown**.

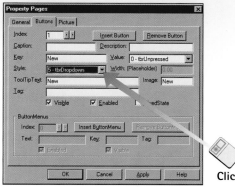

 Click

7 Add the Menu Items

For each button menu item you want, click the **Insert ButtonMenu** button at the bottom of the **Property Pages** and enter the appropriate information.

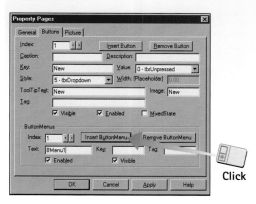

 Click

End

How-To Hints

The Toolbar Wizard

If you are using the Toolbar Wizard to create the toolbar, you should add all of the buttons you need at one time because the wizard adds the **SELECT** code for you.

How to Use the Visual Data Manager

The **Visual Data Manager** is a standalone application that gives you the ability to create and modify database tables and information. In addition, you can use it to add data, display data, and test SQL statements before using them in a Visual Basic application. The **Visual Data Manager** can be started by itself; however, it is also available from the Visual Basic **Add-Ins** menu.

Begin

1 Start the Visual Data Manager

To start the **Visual Data Manager**, pull down the **Add-Ins** menu and choose **Visual Data Manager**.

Click

2 Open a Database

To work with a database, you must open it. In the **Visual Data Manager**, pull down the **File** menu, select **Open Database** and then **Microsoft Access**.

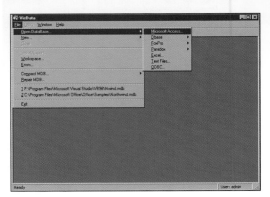

3 Specify the Database File

Locate and select the **Nwind.MDB** database file in the **Open Microsoft Access Database** dialog and click the **Open** button.

4 View the Database Tables

After the database is opened, every table and query is displayed in the **Database Window**.

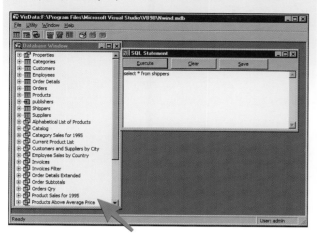

5 Display Data

To display the data in any of the tables or queries, simply double-click it. This will display the data in one of three forms depending on the **Layout** button that is selected.

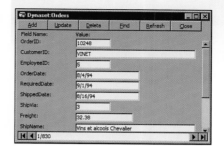

6 Test SQL Statements

To test a SQL statement, enter it in the **SQL Statement** window and click the **Execute** button. This will display the data in the selected layout.

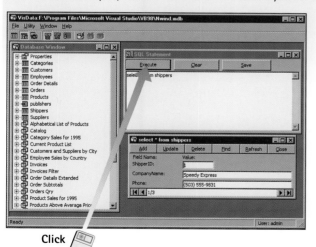

Click

How-To Hints

Creating Test Data

Not only is the Visual Data Manager excellent to use to create the tables and columns in a database, it can also be used to enter data in the database to test for any given type of data that might be entered by the user.

End

How to Use the API Viewer

The **API Viewer** is one of those unsung heroes of Visual Basic. When you start creating larger more complicated applications, you will find that there are times when you need to use a function or action that is just not available in Visual Basic. The collection of APIs is not included with Visual Basic; they are really the backbone of the Windows operating system. In order to use APIs, you need to know which system file they are in and how to define them to Visual Basic. Included with Visual Basic is a file that includes all of the API definitions that you can use. The **API Viewer** displays all of these definitions for you to select from and add to your application.

Begin

1 Start the API Viewer

To start the **API Viewer**, pull down the **Add-Ins** menu and choose **API Viewer**.

Click

2 Load the API file

The first thing you need to do is open the file that contains the API definitions. These definitions can be either in a database file or a text file. Visual Basic includes a text file that contains these definitions. To load this file, in the **API Viewer** choose the **File** menu and select **Load Text File**.

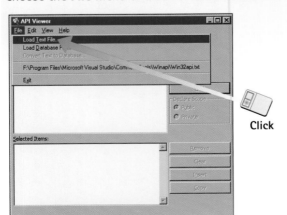

Click

3 Specify the Definition File

Locate and select the **Win32api.TXT** database file and click the **Open** button.

4 Browse the List of APIs

All of the available Windows 32-bit API calls are now listed in the **Available Items** pane. To use them, find the one or ones you need and click the **Add** button.

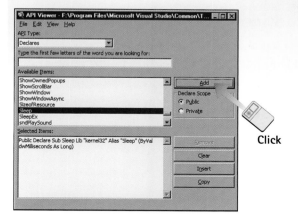

Click

5 Add the Definitions

After you have selected all the APIs you need, you can click the **Insert** button to add them to the current form, or copy them and paste them into the form or module you want.

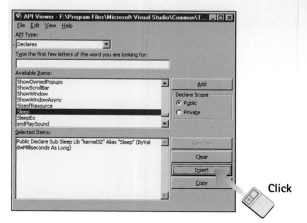

Click

6 Using the API in the Project

The API definitions are now included in your application ready for you to use.

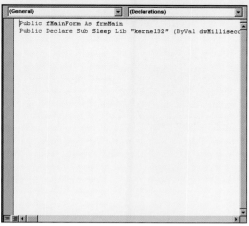

End

How-To Hints

Using APIs

Using API calls in a Visual Basic application requires a certain amount of knowledge about how Windows interacts with Visual Basic and what the different API statements actually do. Before using any API calls, you should learn a little about what they are and how they work.

TASK 7

How to Use the Template Manager

One of the features of Visual Basic is the ability to use templates and forms that have been previously created. The **Template Manager** gives you access to these objects from within Visual Basic on the **Tools** menu. Using the **Template Manager**, you can add sections of code, menu groups, or formatted controls and related code. Each of the three types of templates is added the same way using the **Template Manager**. To add these objects with the **Template Manager** would require you to open the other form or module, copy the controls and/or code, and then paste them onto the new form.

Begin

1 Using the Template Manager

To add a control set to a form, pull down the **Tools** menu and choose **Add Control Set**.

Click

2 Select the Template

From the **Add Control Set** dialog displayed, choose the template you want to use and click **Open**.

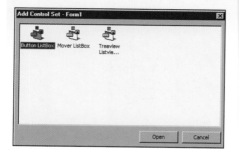

3 Using the New Objects

The template that you selected is then added to your form. You can now add any additional code that you might need.

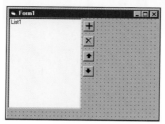

4 Add Additional Templates

You can add your own templates to the **Template Manager** by creating a new form or code and then moving a copy of that form or module file to the related subdirectory on your computer.

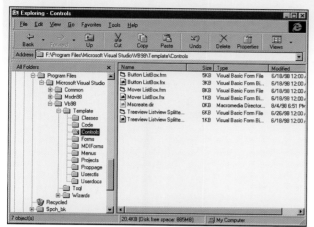

End

How-To Hints

Templates

If you use the same sections of code or designed forms, it would be easier to add them to the **Template Manager** than to look for the files that contain them every time you need to copy them into a new project or form.

What to Watch Out For

Although templates sound like a good idea, it is usually easier just to copy the sections of code or controls from one form to another. Using templates requires you to keep track of the code that is included in them and make any changes to them that might be needed.

Glossary

API (Application Programming Interface) Method that uses the Microsoft Windows resources as part of a Visual Basic application.

APP object A global object that contains information about the application's title, version information, path, and name of its executable file and Help files, and whether a previous instance of the application is running.

Application A complete software program that was designed to perform a certain task or operation such as word processing.

Application Wizard A wizard that is included with Visual Basic that assists you in generating the shell of a complex application using one of the three predefined visual interfaces.

Argument A parameter containing data (characters, numerics, or objects) that is passed to a procedure.

Array A combination of data variables that can be accessed in sequence.

Breakpoint The action of stopping the execution of a program at a predetermined location in the Visual Basic code.

CheckBox control A control that displays True or False values in the form a check. If the checkmark is shown, then the value is True; if it is not shown, then the value is False.

Code The words, numbers, and symbols that make up a computer program.

Code Editor The tool that is used to enter and change the program code.

Collection An object that contains zero or more objects of the same type.

Column A single list of data in a database table. A column can also be referred to as a field.

ComboBox control A control that contains a textbox combined with a drop-down list of allowable values that can be selected.

Command Button control A standard Windows control that will trigger a **Click** event when the user clicks it with the mouse.

Comment A statement in the program code that is ignored by Visual Basic. This is used to provide information to the programmer about what the code is doing.

Common Dialog control The Visual Basic control that displays the standard Windows dialog boxes to open or save a file, change colors or fonts, modify printer options, and display Help.

Compile The process of converting the Visual Basic code into a single executable file that the computer can understand.

Constant A value in a Visual Basic program that is unchanging within the application. Once a constant has been defined, it cannot be modified.

Container   An object that holds other objects.

Control   An object that can be added to a Visual Basic form. A control supports a single task, such as text entry or displaying a label.

Control array   A group of controls that are treated as an array. Each member of the control array can be accessed using an index value.

D

Data Access Objects (DAO)   A collection of objects, methods, and properties that provide access to a specified database. This access method has been largely replaced in Visual Basic 6 with ActiveX Data Objects (ADO).

Database   A collection of structures and other components that were designed to store data efficiently.

Database application   An application that was created to support database processing. This includes database access and the user interface that makes the database easy to use.

Database table   The basic structure in a database. Each table contains rows (records) and columns (fields) of data.

Data Form Wizard   Included with Visual Basic and provides a way to automatically generate Visual Basic forms that contain individual databound controls and procedures used to manage information retrieved from a database.

DateTimePicker control   A control that enables you to provide a formatted date field that allows easy date selection (see **MonthView control**).

Debug Window   The window in the Visual Basic environment that enables you to run and test the program code.

Debugging   The process of finding and fixing errors in the logic of a computer program.

Declaration Section   The area in a code module that contains the module-level variable and constant declarations.

DLL (dynamically linked library)   This is a file that is loaded into memory when needed by an application. A DLL is shared between applications and can contain many different functions and processes that an application might use.

E

ERR object   An object that contains information about a runtime error which can be accessed from within the Visual Basic application.

Executable   A file that can be run outside of the Visual Basic design environment.

Expression   A combination of values, variables, and operators that will provide a unique value.

F-G

Field   A single item of information that is contained in a record of a database table (see **Column**).

Focus   Describes the state of the selected or high-lighted object on the screen. Only one object can contain the focus at a time.

Form   A form is an object that contains controls for displaying and editing data.

Function   See **Procedure**.

H-I-J

Index   A numeric or string reference to a member of an array or collection.

Inputbox   Displays a prompt in a dialog box, waits for the user to enter text or click a button, and then returns the contents of the textbox.

K

Keyboard shortcut   A Windows convention that makes the application easier to use. A keyboard shortcut is a combination of a single character and either the **Ctrl**, **Alt**, or **Shift** key. When pressed together, it will perform a defined action.

Keyword   A word that is used by Visual Basic and cannot be used as the name of an object or variable with the application.

L-M-N

ListBox control   A control that displays a scrolling list of text or numbers.

Menu   A list of items, such as commands and file-names, that appears when you choose a menu option from the menu bar.

Method   A method is attached to an object and defines an action that is supported by the object.

MonthView control   A control that enables you to create applications that allow users to view and set date information via a calendar-like interface (see **DateTimePicker control**).

MsgBox   Displays a message in a dialog box, and then waits for the user to click a button.

O

Object   A unique entity within a Visual Basic application. All forms, controls, and some variables are considered objects.

Object Browser   A reference tool included with Visual Basic that displays the classes, properties, methods, events, and constants available from the object libraries included in the application, as well as the procedures in your project.

ODBC   (Open Database Connectivity) Describes a standard that is used to communicate database sources such as Microsoft SQL Server.

Option Button   A control that provides a method to select from among a set of mutually exclusive values.

P

Parameter   Data that is passed to a procedure (see **Argument**).

Private   A keyword that defines the scope or visibility of a variable within an application. A variable or procedure that is defined as private can only be used within that module or routine.

Procedure   A defined section of code that performs a specific task. There are two types of procedures: functions and subroutines. A function can return a single value to the calling statement, while a subroutine cannot.

Project   The Visual Basic definition that contains the collection of forms, controls, and modules that make up the Visual Basic application.

Property   An attribute of an object.

Public   A keyword that defines the scope or visibility of a variable within an application. A variable or procedure that is defined as public can be used anywhere in the application.

Q-R

Query Used to access data that is stored in a database.

Random file A file type that allows data to be read from and written to it in any order.

Record A single row of data in a database table.

Recordset Defines a set of records that have been retrieved from a database.

Rich TextBox control A control that allows the user to enter and edit text while also providing more advanced formatting features than the conventional TextBox control.

S

Scrollbar A scrollbar is used to provide visual feedback when browsing large amounts of text or changing a relative value of a variable.

Sequential file A file type that stores data in a linear fashion. Each new piece of information is added to the file immediately after the preceding data. When reading data from the file, the program must start at the top of the file and read through all of the data to the end.

Shortcut key See **Keyboard shortcut**.

Source code See **Code**.

Statement A sequence of commands, variables, operators, and Visual Basic keywords that act as a single executable unit.

String A data type that contains only letters of the alphabet, numeric digits, and punctuation marks.

Subroutine See **Procedure**.

Syntax The rules that determine of Visual Basic code can be written.

T-V

Tab control A control that provides a group of tabs, each of which acts as a container for other controls. Only one tab is active in the control at a time, displaying the controls it contains to the user while hiding the controls in the other tabs.

TextBox control A control that is used to display data or accept input from the user.

Timer control A control that is used to perform an action in a program based on the computer's clock.

Toolbar A complex control that contains command buttons that provide the user quick access to many functions of the application.

Toolbar Wizard A wizard that is included with the Application Wizard in Visual Basic, which assists you in creating a **Toolbar** for the application.

Toolbox The Visual Basic dialog that displays the available controls that have been added to the application.

W-X-Y-Z

Variable A name that is used to access a value within an application.

Visual Data Manager An application that was created using Visual Basic and is included to provide database access. This application allows you to create, modify, and view data from a database.

Index

Immediate window, 148
printing variables, 149

implicit variables, 82

Index property, control array, 125

Input statement, 230–231

Inputbox function, 52–53
validating input, 53

insertable objects, 23

installing
MSDN (Microsoft Developers Network) Help software, 10
Visual Basic, 8-9

integer division operator (\), 89

integer variables, 86

interface, 18–19
customizing, 20
Code Editor, 20
controls, adding to toolbox, 22-23
docking dialogs, 21
environment, 21
general settings, 21

Internet Explorer, 9

Interval property, 157

invalid controls, 23

Item property, collections, 123